AVATÂRAS

FOUR LECTURES DELIVERED AT THE TWENTY-FOURTH ANNIVERSARY MEETING OF THE THEOSOPHICAL SOCIETY AT ADYAR, MADRAS, DECEMBER, 1899

BY

ANNIE BESANT

A Yesterday's World Publishing

Published by A Yesterday's World Publishing
Copyright © 2025 A Yesterday's World Publishing
First impression 2025
ISBN - 978-1-916923-61-4

CONTENTS.

FIRST LECTURE.

What is an Avatâra?

BROTHERS:—Every time that we come here together to study the fundamental truths of all religions, I cannot but feel how vast is the subject, how small the expounder, how mighty the horizon that opens before our thoughts, how narrow the words which strive to sketch it for your eyes. Year after year we meet, time after time we strive to fathom some of those great mysteries of life, of the Self, which form the only subject really worthy of the profoundest thought of man. All else is passing; all else is transient; all else is but the toy of a moment. Fame and power, wealth and science—all that is in this world below is as nothing beside the grandeur of the Eternal Self in the universe and in man, one in all His manifold manifestations, marvellous and beautiful in every form that He puts forth. And this year, of all the manifestations of the Supreme, we are going to dare to study the holiest of the holiest, those manifestations of God in the world in which He shows Himself as divine, coming to help the world that He has made, shining forth in His essential nature, the form but a thin film which scarce veils the Divinity from our eyes. How then shall we venture to approach it, how shall we dare to study it, save with deepest reverence, with profoundest humility; for if there needs for the study of His works patience, reverence and humbleness of heart, what when we study Him whose works but partially reveal Him, when we try to understand what is meant by an Avatâra, what is the meaning, what the purpose of such a revelation?

Our President has truly said that in all the faiths of the world there is belief in such manifestations, and that ancient maxim as to truth—that which is as the hall mark on the silver showing that the metal is pure—that ancient maxim is here valid, that whatever has been believed everywhere, whatever has been believed at every time, and by every one, that is true, that is reality. Religions quarrel over many details; men dispute over many propositions; but where human heart and human voice speak a single word, there you have the mark of truth, there you have the sign of spiritual reality. But in dealing with the subject one difficulty faces us, faces you as hearers, faces myself as speaker. In every religion in modern times truth is shorn of her full proportions; the intellect alone cannot grasp the many aspects of the one truth. So we have school after school, philosophy after philosophy, each one showing an aspect of truth, and ignoring, or even denying, the other aspects which are equally true. Nor is this all; as the age in which we are passes on from century to century, from millennium to millennium, knowledge becomes dimmer, spiritual insight becomes rarer, those who repeat far out-number those who know; and those who speak with clear vision of the spiritual verity are lost amidst the crowds, who only hold traditions whose origin they fail to understand. The priest and the prophet, to use two well-known words, have ever in later times come into conflict one with the other. The priest carries on the traditions of antiquity; too often he has lost the knowledge that made them real. The prophet—coming forth from time to time with the divine word hot as fire on his lips—speaks out the ancient truth and illuminates tradition. But they who cling to the words of tradition are apt to be blinded by the light of the fire and to call out "heretic" against the one who speaks the truth that they have lost. Therefore, in religion after religion, when some great teacher has arisen, there have been opposition, clamour, rejection, because the truth he spoke was too mighty to be narrowed within the limits of half-blinded men. And in such a subject as we are to study to-day, certain grooves have been made, certain ruts as it were, in which the human mind is running, and I know that in laying before you the occult truth, I must needs, at some points, come into clash with details of a tradition that is rather repeated by memory than either understood or the truths beneath it grasped. Pardon me then, my brothers, if in a speech on this great topic I should sometimes come athwart some of the dividing lines of different schools of Hindu thought; I may not, I dare not, narrow the truth I have learnt, to suit the limitations that have grown up by the ignorance of ages, nor make that which is the spiritual verity conform to the empty traditions that are left in the faiths of the world. By the duty laid upon me by the Master that I serve, by the truth that He has bidden me speak in the ears of men of all the faiths that are in this modern world; by these I must tell you what is true, no matter whether or not you agree with it for the moment; for the truth that is spoken wins submission afterwards, if not at the moment; and any one who speaks of the Ṛishis of antiquity must speak the truths that they taught in their days, and not repeat the mere commonplaces of commentators of modern times and the petty orthodoxies that ring us in on every side and divide man from man.

I propose in order to simplify this great subject to divide it under certain heads. I propose first to remind you of the two great divisions recognised by all who have thought on the subject; then to take up especially, for this morning, the question, "What is an Avatâra?" To-morrow we shall put and strive to answer, partly at least, the question, "Who is the source of Avatâras?" Then later we shall take up special Avatâras both of the kosmos and of human races. Thus I hope to place before you a clear, definite succession of ideas on this great subject, not asking you to believe them because I speak them, not asking you to accept them because I utter them. Your reason is the bar to which every truth must come which is true for you; and you err deeply, almost fatally, if you let the voice of authority impose itself where you do not answer to the speaking. Every truth is only true to you as you see it, and as it illuminates the mind; and truth however true is not yet truth for you, unless your heart opens out to receive it, as the flower opens out its heart to receive the rays of the morning sun.

First, then, let us take a statement that men of every religion will accept. Divine manifestations of a special kind take place from time to time as the need arises for their appearance; and these special manifestations are marked out from the universal manifestation of God in His kosmos; for never forget that in the lowest creature that crawls the earth I'shvara is present as in the highest Deva. But there are certain special manifestations marked out from this general self-revelation in the kosmos, and it is these special manifestations which are called forth by special needs. Two words especially have been used in Hinduism, marking a certain distinction in the nature of the manifestation—one the word "Avatâra," the other the word "A´vesha." Only for a moment need we stop on the meaning of the words, important to us because the literal meaning of the words points to the fundamental difference between the two. The word "Avatâra," as you know, has as its root "tṛi," passing over, and with the prefix which is added, the "ava," you get the idea of descent, one who descends. That is the literal meaning of the word. The other word has as its root "viṣh," permeating, penetrating, pervading, and you have there the thought of something which is permeated or penetrated. So that while in the one case, Avatâra, there is the thought of a descent from above, from I'shvara to man or animal; in the other, there is rather the idea of an entity already existing who is influenced, permeated, pervaded by the divine power, specially illuminated as it were. And thus we have a kind of intermediate step, if one may say so, between the divine manifestation in the Avatâra and in the kosmos—the partial divine manifestation in one who is permeated by the influence of the Supreme, or of some other being who practically dominates the individual, the Ego who is thus permeated.

Now what are the occasions which lead to these great manifestations? None can speak with mightier authority on this point than He who came Himself as an Avatâra just before the beginning of our own age, the Divine Lord Shrî Kṛiṣhṇa Himself. Turn to that marvellous poem, the *Bhagavad-Gîtâ*, to the fourth Adhyâya, Shlokas 7 and 8; there He tells us what draws Him forth to birth into His world in the manifested form of the Supreme:

यदा यदाहिधर्मस्य ग्लानिर्भवति भारत ।
अभ्युत्थानमधर्मस्य तदात्मानं सृजाम्यहम् ॥
परित्राणाय साधूनां विनाशायचदुष्कृतां ।
धर्मसंस्थापनार्थाय सम्भवामि युगेयुगे ॥

"When Dharma,—righteousness, law—decays, when Adharma—unrighteousness, lawlessness—is exalted, then I Myself come forth: for the protection of the good, for the destruction of the evil, for the establishing firmly of Dharma, I am born from age to age." That is what He tells us of the coming forth of the Avatâra. That is, the needs of His world call upon Him to manifest Himself in His divine power; and we know from other of His sayings that in addition to those which deal with the human needs, there are certain kosmic necessities which in the earlier ages of the world's story called forth special manifestations. When in the great wheel of evolution another turn round has to be given, when some new form, new type of life is coming forth, then also the Supreme reveals Himself, embodying the type which thus He initiates in His kosmos, and in this way turning that everlasting wheel which He comes forth as I'shvara to turn. Such then, speaking quite generally, the meaning of the word, and the object of the coming.

From that we may fitly turn to the more special question, "What is an Avatâra?" And it is here that I must ask your close attention, nay, your patient consideration, where points that to some extent may be unfamiliar are laid before you; for as I said, it is the occult view of the truth which I am going to partially unveil, and those who have not thus studied truth need to think carefully ere they reject, need to consider long ere they refuse. We shall see as we try to answer the question how far the great authorities help us to understand, and how far the lack of knowledge in reading those authorities has led to misconception. You may remember that the late learned T. Subba Rao in the lectures that he gave on the *Bhagavad-Gîtâ* put to you a certain view of the Avatâra, that it was a descent of I'shvara—or, as he said, using the theosophical term, the Logos, which is only the Greek name for I'shvara—a descent of I'shvara, uniting Himself with a human soul. With all respect for the profound learning of the lamented pandit, I cannot but think that that is only a partial definition. Probably he did not at that time desire, had not very possibly the time, to deal with case after case, having so wide a field to cover in the small number of lectures that he gave, and he therefore chose out one form, as we may say, of self-revelation, leaving untouched the others, which now in dealing with the subject by itself we have full time to study. Let me then begin as it were at the beginning, and then give you certain authorities which may make the view easier to accept; let me state without any kind of attempt to veil or evade, what is really an Avatâra. Fundamentally He is the result of evolution. In far past Kalpas, in worlds other than this, nay, in universes earlier than our own, those who were to be Avatâras climbed slowly, step by step, the vast ladder of evolution, climbing from mineral to plant, from plant to animal, from animal to man, from man to Jîvanmukta, from Jîvanmukta higher and higher yet, up the mighty hierarchy that stretches beyond Those who have liberated Themselves from the bonds of humanity; until at last, thus climbing, They cast off not only all the limits of the separated Ego, not only burst asunder the limitations of the separated Self, but entered I´shvara Himself and expanded into the all-consciousness of the Lord, becoming one in knowledge as they had ever been one in essence with that eternal Life from which originally they came forth, living in that life, centres without circumferences, living centres, one with the Supreme. There stretches behind such a One the endless chain of birth after birth, of manifestation after manifestation. During the stage in which He was human, during the long climbing up of the ladder of humanity, there were two special characteristics that marked out the future Avatâra from the ranks of men. One his absolute bhakti, his devotion to the Supreme; for only those who are bhaktas and who to their bhakti have wed gnyâna, or knowledge, can reach this goal; for by devotion, says Shrî Kṛiṣhṇa, can a man "enter into My being." And the need of the devotion for the future Avatâra is this: he must keep the centre that he has built even in the life of I´shvara, so that he may be able to draw the circumference once again round that centre, in order that he may come forth as a manifestation of I'shvara, one with Him in knowledge, one with Him in power, the very Supreme Himself in earthly life; he must hence have the power of limiting himself to form, for no form can exist in the universe save as there is a centre within it round which that form is drawn. He must be so devoted as to be willing to remain for the service of the universe while I´shvara Himself abides in it, to share the continual sacrifice made by Him, the sacrifice whereby the universe lives. But not devotion alone marks this great One who is climbing his divine path. He must also be, as I´shvara is, a lover of humanity. Unless within him there burns the flame of love for men—nay, men, do I say? it is too narrow—unless within him burns the flame of love for everything that exists, moving and unmoving, in this universe of God, he will not be able to come forth as the Supreme whose life and love are in everything that He has brought forth out of His eternal and inexhaustible life. "There is nothing," says the Beloved, "moving or unmoving, that may exist bereft of me;"[1] and unless the man can work that into his nature, unless he can love everything that is, not only the beautiful but the ugly, not only the good but the evil, not only the attractive but the repellent, unless in every form he sees the Self,

[1] *Bhagavad-Gîtâ*, x. 39.

he cannot climb the steep path the Avatâra must tread.

These, then, are the two great characteristics of the man who is to become the special manifestation of God—bhakti, love to the One in whom he is to merge, and love to those whose very life is the life of God. Only as these come forth in the man is he on the path that leads him to be—in future universes, in far, far future kalpas—an Avatâra coming as God to man.

Now on this view of the nature of an Avatâra difficulties, I know, arise; but they are difficulties that arise from a partial view, and then from that view having been merely accepted, as a rule, on the authority of some great name, instead of on the thinking out and thorough understanding of it by the man who repeats the shibboleth of his own sect or school. The view once taken, every text in Shruti or Smṛiti that goes against that view is twisted out of its natural meaning, in order to be made to agree with the idea which already dominates the mind. That is the difficulty with every religion; a man acquires his view by tradition, by habit, by birth, by public opinion, by the surroundings of his own time and of his own day. He finds in the scriptures—which belong to no time, to no day, to no one age, and to no one people, but are expressions of the eternal Veda—he finds in them many texts that do not fit into the narrow framework that he has made; and because he too often cares for the framework more than for the truth, he manipulates the text until he can make it fit in, in some dislocated fashion; and the ingenuity of the commentator too often appears in the skill with which he can make words appear to mean what they do not mean in their grammatical and obvious sense. Thus, men of every school, under the mighty names of men who knew the truth—but who could only give such portion of truth as they deemed man at the time was able to receive—use their names to buttress up mistaken interpretations, and thus walls are continually built up to block the advancing life of man.

Now let me take one example from one of the greatest names, one who knew the truth he spoke, but also, like every teacher, had to remember that while he was man, those to whom he spoke were children that could not grasp truth with virile understanding. That great teacher, founder of one of the three schools of the Vedânta, Shrî Râmânujâchârya, in his commentary on the *Bhagavad-Gîtâ*—a priceless work which men of every school might read and profit by—dealing with the phrase in which Shrî Kṛiṣhṇa declares that He has had

बहूनि जन्मानि

"many births," points out how vast the variety of those births had been. Then, confining himself to His manifestations as I´shvara—that is after He had attained to the Supreme—he says quite truly that He was born by His own will; not by karma that compelled Him, not by any force outside Him that coerced Him, but by His own will He came forth as I'shvara and incarnated in one form or another. But there is nothing said there of the innumerable steps traversed by the mighty One ere yet He merged Himself in the Supreme. Those are left on one side, unmentioned, unnoticed, because what the writer had in his view was to present to the hearts of men a great Object for adoration, who might gradually lift them upwards and upwards until the Self should blossom in them in turn. No word is said of the previous kalpas, of the universes stretching backward into the illimitable past. He speaks of His birth as Deva, as Nâga, as Gandharva, as those many shapes that He has taken by His own will. As you know, or as you may learn if you turn to *Shrîmad-Bhâgavata*, there is a much longer list of manifestations than the ten usually called Avatâras. There are given one after another the forms which seem strange to the superficial reader when connected in modern thought with the Supreme. But we find light thrown on the question by some other words of the great Lord; and we also find in one famous book, full of occult hints—though not with much explanation of the hints given—the *Yoga Vâsishtha*, a clear definite statement that the deities, as Mahâdeva, Vishṇu and Brahmâ, have all climbed upward to the mighty posts They hold.[1] And that may well be so, if you think of it; there is nothing derogatory to Them in the thought; for there is but one Existence, the eternal fount of all that comes forth as separated, whether separated in the universe as I'shvara, or separated in the copy of the universe in man; there is but One without a second; there is no life but His, no independence but His, no self-existence but His, and from Him Gods and men and all take their root and exist for ever in and by His one eternal life. Different stages of manifestation, but the One Self in all the different stages, the One living in all; and if it be true, as true it is, that the Self in man is

अजो नित्यः शाश्वतोऽयंपुराणो

"unborn, constant, eternal, ancient," it is because the Self in man is one with the One Self-existent, and I'shvara Himself is only the mightiest manifestation of that One who knows no second near Himself. Says an English poet:

> Closer is He than breathing, nearer than hands and feet.

The Self is in you and in me, as much as the Self is in I'shvara, that One, eternal, unchanging, undecaying, whereof every manifested existence is but one ray of glory. Thus it is true, that which is taught in the *Yoga Vâsishtha*; true it is that even the greatest, before whom we bow in worship, has climbed in ages past all human reckoning to be one with the Supreme, and, ever there, to manifest Himself as God to the world.

But now we come to a distinction that we find made, and it is a real one. We read of a Pûrṇâvatâra, a full, complete, Avatâra. What is the meaning of that word "full" as applied to the Avatâra? The name is given, as we know, to Shrî Kṛishṇa. He is marked out specially by that name. Truly the word "pûrṇa" cannot apply to the Illimitable, the Infinite; He may not be shown forth in any form; the eye may never behold Him; only the spirit that is Himself can know the One. What is meant by it is that, so far as is possible within the limits of form, the manifestation of the formless appears, so far as is possible it came forth in that great One who came for the helping of the world. This may assist you to grasp the distinction. Where the manifestation is that of a Pûrṇâvatâra, then at any moment of time, at His own will, by Yoga or otherwise, He can transcend every limit of the form in which He binds Himself by His own will, and shine forth as the Lord of the Universe, within whom all the Universe is contained. Think for a moment once more of Shrî Kṛishṇa, who teaches us so much on this. Turn to that great storehouse of spiritual wisdom, the *Mahâbhârata*, to the Ashvamedha Parva which contains the Anugîtâ, and you will find that Arjuṇa after the great battle, forgetting the teaching that was given him on Kurukshetra, asked his Teacher to repeat that teaching once again.

---

[1] Part II., Chapter ii., Shlokas 14, 15, 16.

And Shrî Kṛishṇa, rebuking him for the fickleness of his mind and stating that He was much displeased that such knowledge should by fickleness have been forgotten, uttered these remarkable words: "It is not possible for me to state it in full in that way. I discoursed to thee on the Supreme Brahman, having concentrated myself in Yoga." And then He goes on to give out the essence of that teaching, but not in the same sublime form as we have it in the *Bhagavad-Gîtâ*. That is one thing that shows you what is meant by a Pûrṇâvatâra; in a condition of Yoga, into which He throws Himself at will, He knows Himself as Lord of everything, as the Supreme on whom the Universe is built. Nay more; thrice at least—I am not sure if there may have been more cases, but if so I cannot at the moment remember them—thrice at least during His life as Shrî Kṛishṇa He shows himself forth as I'shvara, the Supreme. Once in the court of Dhritarâshṭra, when the madly foolish Duryodhana talked about imprisoning within cell-walls the universal Lord whom the universe cannot confine; and to show the wild folly of the arrogant prince, out in the court before every eye He shone forth as Lord of all, filling earth and sky with His glory, and all forms human and divine, superhuman and subhuman, were seen gathered round Him in the life from which they spring. Then on Kurukshetra to Arjuna, His beloved disciple, to whom He gave the divine vision that he might see Him in His Vaiṣhṇava form, the form of Viṣhṇu, the Supreme Upholder of the Universe. And later, on his way back to Dvârakâ, meeting with Utanka, He and the sage came to a misunderstanding, and the sage was preparing to curse the Lord; to save him from the folly of uttering a curse against the Supreme, as a child might throw a tiny pebble against a rock of immemorial age, He shone out before the eyes of him who was really His bhakta, and showed him the great Vaiṣhṇava form, that of the Supreme. What do those manifestations show? that at will He can show himself forth as Lord of all, casting aside the limits of human form in which men live; casting aside the appearance so familiar to those around Him, He could reveal himself as the mighty One, I'shvara who is the life of all. There is the mark of a Pûrṇâvatâra; always within His grasp, at will, is the power to show Himself forth as I'shvara.

But why—the thought may arise in your minds—are not all Avatâras of this kind, since all are verily of the Supreme Lord? The answer is that by His own will, by his own Mâyâ, He veils Himself within the limits which serve the creatures whom He has come to help. Ah, how different He is, this Mighty One, from you and me! When we are talking to some one who knows a little less than ourselves, we talk out all we know to show our knowledge, expanding ourselves as much as we can so as to astonish and make marvel the one to whom we speak; that is because we are so small that we fear our greatness will not be recognised unless we make ourselves as large as we can to astonish, if possible to terrify; but when He comes who is really great, who is mightier than anything which He produces, He makes Himself small in order to help those whom He loves. And do you know, my brothers, that only in proportion as His spirit enters into us, can we in our little measure be helpers in the universe of which He is the one life; until we, in all our doings and speakings, place ourselves within the one we want to help and not outside him, feeling as he feels, thinking as he thinks, knowing for the time as he knows, with all his limitations, although there may be further knowledge beyond, we cannot truly help; that is the condition of all true help given by man to man, as it is the only condition of the help which is given to man by God Himself.

And so in other Avatâras, He limits Himself for men's sake. Take the great king, Shrî Râma. What did he come to show? The ideal Kshattriya, in every relation of the Kshattriya life; as son—perfect as son alike to loving father and to jealous and for the time unkind step-mother. For you may remember that when the father's wife who was not His own mother bade him go forth to the forest on the very eve of His coronation as heir, His gentle answer was: "Mother, I go." Perfect as son. Perfect as husband; if He had not limited Himself by His own will to show out what husband should be to wife, how could He in the forest, when Sîtâ had been reft away by Râvana, have shown the grief, have uttered the piteous lamentations, which have drawn tears from thousands of eyes, as He calls on plants and on trees, on animals and birds, on Gods and men, to tell Him where His wife, His other self, the life of His life, had gone? How could he have taught men what wife should be to husband's heart unless He had limited Himself? The consciously Omnipresent Deity could not seek and search for His beloved who had disappeared. And then as king; as perfect king as He was perfect son and husband. When the welfare of His subjects was concerned, when the safety of the realm was to be thought of, when He remembered that He as king stood for God and must be perfect in the eyes of His subjects, so that they might give the obedience and the loyalty, which men can only give to one whom they know as greater than themselves, then even His wife was put aside; then the test of the fire for Sîtâ, the unsullied and the suffering; then She must pass through it to show that no sin or pollution had come upon Her by the foul touch of Râvana, the Râkshasa; then the demand that ere husband's heart that had been riven might again clasp the wife, She must come forth pure as woman; and all this, because He was king as well as husband, and on the throne the people honoured as divine there must only be purity, spotless as driven snow. Those limitations were needed in order that a perfect example might be given to man, and man might learn to climb by reproducing virtues, made small in order that his small grasp might hold them.

We come to the second great class of manifestations, that to which I alluded in the beginning as covered by the wide term A′vesha. In that case it is not that a man in past universes has climbed upward and has become one with I′shvara; but it is that a man has climbed so far as to become so great, so perfect in his manhood, and so full of love and devotion to God and man, that God is able to permeate him with a portion of His own influence, His own power, His own knowledge, and send him forth into the world as a superhuman manifestation of Himself. The individual Ego remains; that is the great distinction. The *man* is there, though the power that is acting is the manifested God. Therefore the manifestation will be coloured by the special characteristics of the one over whom this overshadowing is made; and you will be able to trace in the thoughts of this inspired teacher, the characteristics of the race, of the individual, of the form of knowledge which belongs to that man in the incarnation in which the great overshadowing takes place. That is the fundamental difference.

But here we find that we come at once to endless grades, endless varieties, and down the ladder of lesser and lesser evolution we may tread, step by step, until we come to the lower grades that we call inspiration. In a case of A′vesha it generally continues through a great portion of the life, the latter portion, as a rule, and it is comparatively seldom withdrawn. Inspiration, as generally understood, is a more partial thing, more temporary. Divine power comes down, illuminates and irradiates the man for the moment, and he speaks for the time with authority, with knowledge, which in his normal state he will be unable probably to compass. Such are the prophets who have illuminated the world age after age; such were in ancient days the Brâhmaṇas who were the mouth of God. Then truly the distinction was not that I spoke of between priest and prophet; both were joined in the one illumination, and the teaching of the priest and the preaching of the prophet ran on the same lines and gave forth the same great truths. But in later times the distinction arose by the failure of the priesthood, when the priest turned aside for money, for fame, for power, for all the things with which only younger souls ought to concern themselves—human toys with which human babies play, and do wisely in so playing, for they grow by them. Then the priests became formal, the prophets became more and more rare, until the great fact of inspiration was thrown back wholly into the past, as though God or man had altered, man no longer divine in his nature, God no longer willing to speak words in the ears of men. But inspiration is a fact in all its stages; and it goes far farther than some of you may think. The inspiration of the prophets, spiritually mighty and convincing, is needed, and they come to the world to give a new impulse to spiritual truth. But there is a general inspiration that any one may share who strives to show out the divine life from which no son of man is excluded, for every son of man is son of God. Have you ever been drawn away for a moment into higher, more peaceful realms, when you have come across something of beauty, of art, of the wonders of science, of the grandeur of philosophy? Have you for a time lost sight of the pettinesses of earth, of trivial troubles, of small worries and annoyances, and felt yourself lifted into a calmer region, into a light that is not the light of common earth? Have you ever stood before some wondrous picture wherein the palette of the painter has been taxed to light the canvas with all the hues of beauteous colour that art can give to human sight? Or have you seen in some wondrous sculpture, the gracious living curves that the chisel has freed from the roughness of the marble? Or have you listened while the diviner spell of music has lifted you, step by step, till you seem to hear the Gandharvas singing and almost the divine flute is being played and echoing in the lower world? Or have you stood on the mountain peak with the snows around you, and felt the grandeur of the unmoving nature that shows out God as well as the human spirit? Ah, if you have known any of these peaceful spots in life's desert, then you know how all-pervading is inspiration; how wondrous the beauty and the power of God shown forth in man and in the world; then you know, if you never knew it before, the truth of that great proclamation of Shrî Kṛiṣhṇa the Beloved: "Whatever is royal, good, beautiful, and mighty, understand thou that to go forth from My Splendour";[1] all is the reflection of that tejas[2] which is His and His alone. For as there is nought in the universe without His love and life, so there is no beauty that is not His beauty, that is not a ray of the illimitable splendour, one little beam from the unfailing source of life.

---

[1] *Bhagavad-Gîtâ*, x. 41.

[2] Splendour, radiance.

SECOND LECTURE.

The Source of and Need for Avatâras

BROTHERS:—You will remember that yesterday, in dividing the subject under different heads, I put down certain questions which we would take in order. We dealt yesterday with the question: "What is an Avatâra?" The second question that we are to try to answer, "What is the source of Avatâras?" is a question that leads us deep into the mysteries of the kosmos, and needs at least an outline of kosmic growth and evolution in order to give an intelligible answer. I hope to-day to be able also to deal with the succeeding question, "How does the need for Avatâras arise?" This will leave us for to-morrow the subject of the special Avatâras, and I shall endeavour, if possible, during to-morrow's discourse, to touch on nine of the Avatâras out of the ten recognised as standing out from all other manifestations of the Supreme. Then, if I am able to accomplish that task, we shall still have one morning left, and that I propose to give entirely to the study of the greatest of the Avatâras, the Lord Shrî Kṛiṣhṇa Himself, endeavouring, if possible, to mark out the great characteristics of His life and His work, and, it may be, to meet and answer some of the objections of the ignorant which, especially in these later days, have been levelled against Him by those who understand nothing of His nature, nothing of the mighty work He came to accomplish in the world.

Now we are to begin to-day by seeking an answer to the question, "What is the source of Avatâras?" and it is likely that I am going to take a line of thought somewhat unfamiliar, carrying us, as it does, outside the ordinary lines of our study which deals more with the evolution of man, of the spiritual nature within him. It carries us to those far off times, almost incomprehensible to us, when our universe was coming into manifestation, when its very foundations, as it were, were being laid. In answering the question, however, the mere answer is simple. It is recognised in all religions admitting divine incarnations—and they include the great religions the world—it is admitted that the source of Avatâras, the source of the Divine incarnations, is the second or middle manifestation of the sacred Triad. It matters not whether with Hindus we speak of the Trimûrti, or whether with Christians we speak of the Trinity, the fundamental idea is one and the same. Taking first for a moment the Christian symbology, you will find that every Christian tells you that the one divine incarnation acknowledged in Christianity—for in Christianity they believe in one special incarnation only—you will find in the Christian nomenclature the divine incarnation or Avatâra is that of the second person of the Trinity. No Christian will tell you that there has ever been an incarnation of God the Father, the primeval Source of life. They will never tell you that there has been an incarnation of the third Person of the Trinity, the Holy Spirit, the Spirit of Wisdom, of creative Intelligence, who built up the world-materials. But they will always say that it was the second Person, the Son, who took human form, who appeared under the likeness of humanity, who was manifested as man for helping the salvation of the world. And if you analyse what is meant by that phrase, what, to the mind of the Christian, is conveyed by the thought of the second Person of the Trinity—for remember in dealing with a religion that is not yours you should seek for the thought not the form, you should look at the idea not at the label, for the thoughts are universal while the forms divide, the ideas are identical while the labels are marks of separation—if you seek for the underlying thought you will find it is this: the sign of the second Person of the Trinity is duality; also, He is the underlying life of the world; by His power the worlds were made, and are sustained, supported, and protected. You will find that while the Spirit of Wisdom is spoken of as bringing order out of disorder, kosmos out of chaos, that it is by the manifested Word of God, or the second Person of the Trinity, it is by Him that all forms are builded up in this world, and it is specially in His image that man is made. So also when we turn to what will be more familiar to the vast majority of you, the symbology of Hinduism, you will find that all Avatâras have their source in Viṣhṇu, in Him who pervades the universe, as the very name Viṣhṇu implies, who is the Supporter, the Protector, the pervading, all-permeating Life by which the universe is held together, and by which it is sustained. Taking the names of the Trimûrti so familiar to us all—not the philosophical names Sat, Chit, A′nanda, those names which in philosophy show the attributes of the Supreme Brahman—taking the concrete idea, we have Mahâdeva or Shiva, Viṣhṇu, and Brahmâ: three names, just as in the other religion we have three names; but the same fact comes out, that it is the middle or central one of the Three who is the source of Avatâras. There has never been a direct Avatâra of Mahâdeva, of Shiva Himself. Appearances? Yes. Manifestations? Yes. Coming in form for a special purpose served by that form? Oh yes. Take the *Mahâbhârata*, and you find Him appearing in the form of the hunter, the Kirâta, and testing the intuition of Arjuna, and struggling with him to test his strength, his courage, and finally his devotion to Himself. But that is a mere form taken for a purpose and cast aside the moment the purpose is served; almost, we may say, a mere illusion, produced to serve a special purpose and then thrown away as having completed that which it was intended to perform. Over and over again you find such appearances of Mahâdeva. You may remember one most beautiful story, in which He appears in the form of a Chandâla[1] at the gateway of His own city of Kâshî, when one who was especially overshadowed by a manifestation of Himself, Shrî Shankarâchârya, was coming with his disciples to the sacred city; veiling Himself in the form of an outcaste—for to Him all forms are the same, the human differences are but as the grains of sand which vanish before the majesty of His greatness—He rolled Himself in the dust before the gateway, so that the great teacher could not walk across without touching Him, and he called to the Chandâla to make way in order that the Brâhmaṇa might go on unpolluted by the touch of the outcaste; then the Lord, speaking through the form He had chosen, rebuked the very one whom His power overshadowed, asking him questions which he could not answer and thus abasing his pride and teaching him humility. Such forms truly He has taken, but these are not what we can call Avatâras; mere passing forms, not manifestations upon earth where a life is lived and a great drama is played out. So with Brahmâ; He also has appeared from time to time, has manifested Himself for some special purpose; but there is no Avatâra of Brahmâ, which we can speak of by that very definite and well understood term.

Now for this fact there must be some reason. Why is it that we do not find the source of Avatâras alike in all these great divine manifestations? Why do they come from only one aspect and that the aspect of Viṣhṇu? I need not remind you that there is but one Self, and that these names we use are the names of the aspects

[1] An outcaste, equivalent to a scavenger.

that are manifested by the Supreme; we must not separate them so much as to lose sight of the underlying unity. For remember how, when a worshipper of Viṣhṇu had a feeling in his heart against a worshipper of Mahâdeva, as he bowed before the image of Hari, the face of the image divided itself in half, and Shiva or Hara appeared on one side and Viṣhṇu or Hari appeared on the other, and the two, smiling as one face on the bigoted worshipper, told him that Mahâdeva and Viṣhṇu were but one. But in Their functions a division arises; They manifest along different lines, as it were, in the kosmos and for the helping of man; not for Him but for us, do these lines of apparent separateness arise.

Looking thus at it, we shall be able to find the answer to our question, not only who is the source of Avatâras, but why Viṣhṇu is the source. And it is here that I come to the unfamiliar part where I shall have to ask for your special attention as regards the building of the universe. Now I am using the word "universe," in the sense of our solar system. There are many other systems, each of them complete in itself, and, therefore, rightly spoken of as a kosmos, a universe. But each of these systems in its turn is part of a mightier system, and our sun, the centre of our own system, though it be in very truth the manifested physical body of I′shwara Himself, is not the only sun. If you look through the vast fields of space, myriads of suns are there, each one the centre of its own system, of its own universe; and our sun, supreme to us, is but, as it were, a planet in a vaster system, its orbit curved round a sun greater than itself. So in turn that sun, round which our sun is circling, is planet to a yet mightier sun, and each set of systems in its turn circles round a more central sun, and so on—we know not how far may stretch the chain that to us is illimitable; for who is able to plumb the depths and heights of space, or to find a manifested circumference which takes in all universes! Nay, we say that they are infinite in number, and that there is no end to the manifestations of the one Life.

Now that is true physically. Look at the physical universe with the eye of spirit, and you see in it a picture of the spiritual universe. A great word was spoken by one of the Masters or Ṛishis, whom in this Society we honour and whose teachings we follow. Speaking to one of His disciples, or pupils, He rebuked him, because, He said in words never to be forgotten by those who have read them: "You always look at the things of the spirit with the eyes of the flesh. What you ought to do is to look at the things of the flesh with the eyes of the spirit." Now, what does that mean? It means that instead of trying to degrade the spiritual and to limit it within the narrow bounds of the physical, and to say of the spiritual that it cannot be because the human brain is unable clearly to grasp it, we ought to look at the physical universe with a deeper insight and see in it the image, the shadow, the reflection of the spiritual world, and learn the spiritual verities by studying the images that exist of them in the physical world around us. The physical world is easier to grasp. Do not think the spiritual is modelled on the physical; the physical is fundamentally modelled on the spiritual, and if you look at the physical with the eye of spirit, then you find that it is the image of the higher, and then you are able to grasp the higher truth by studying the faint reflections that you see in the world around you. That is what I ask you to do now. Just as you have your sun and suns, many universes, each one part of a system mightier than itself, so in the spiritual universe there is hierarchy beyond hierarchy of spiritual intelligences who are as the suns of the spiritual world. Our physical system has at its centre the great spiritual Intelligence manifested as a Trinity, the I'shvara of that system. Then beyond Him there is a mightier I'shvara, round whom Those who are on the level of the I'shvara of our system circle, looking to Him as Their central life. And beyond Him yet another, and beyond Him others and others yet, until as the physical universes are beyond our thinking, the spiritual hierarchy stretches also beyond our thought, and, dazzled and blinded by the splendour, we sink back to earth, as Arjuna was blinded when the Vaiṣhṇava form shone forth on him, and we cry: "Oh! show us again Thy more limited form that we may know it and live by it. We are not yet ready for the mightier manifestations. We are blinded, not helped, by such blaze of divine splendour."

And so we find that if we would learn we must limit ourselves—nay, we must try to expand ourselves—to the limits of our own system. Why? I have met people who have not really any grasp of this little world, this grain of dust in which they live, who cannot be content unless you answer questions about the One Existence, the Para-Brahma, whom sages revere in silence, not daring to speak even with illuminated mind that knows nirvânic life and has expanded to nirvânic consciousness. The more ignorant the man, the more he thinks he can grasp. The less he understands, the more he resents being told that there are some things beyond the grasp of his intellect, existences so mighty that he cannot even dream of the lowest of the attributes that mark them out. And for myself, who know myself ignorant, who know that many an age must pass ere I shall be able to think of dealing with these profounder problems, I sometimes gauge the ignorance of the questioner by the questions that he asks as to the ultimate existences, and when he wants to know what he calls the primary origin, I know that he has not even grasped the one-thousandth part of the origin out of which he himself has sprung. Therefore, I say to you frankly that these mighty Ones whom we worship are the Gods of our system; beyond them there stretch mightier Ones yet, whom, perhaps, myriads of kalpas hence, we may begin to understand and worship.

Let us then confine ourselves to our own system and be glad if we can catch some ray of the glory that illumines it. Viṣhṇu has His own functions, as also have Brahmâ and Mahâdeva. The first work in this system is done by the third of the sacred great Ones of the Trimûrti, Brahmâ, as you all know, for you have read that there came forth the creative Intelligence as the third of the divine manifestations. I care not what is the symbology you take; perchance that of the *Viṣhṇu Purâṇa* will be most familiar, wherein the unmanifested Viṣhṇu is beneath the water, standing as the first of the Trimûrti, then the Lotus, standing as the second, and the opened Lotus showing Brahmâ, the third, the creative Mind. You may remember that the work of creation began with His activity. When we study from the occult standpoint in what that activity consisted, we find it consisted in impregnating with His own life the matter of the solar system; that He gave His own life to build up form after form of atom, to make the great divisions in the kosmos; that He formed, one after another, the five kinds of matter. Working by His mind—He is sometimes spoken of as Mahat, the great One, Intelligence—He formed Tattvas one after another. Tattvas, you may remember from last year, are the foundations of the atoms, and there are five of them manifested at the present time. That is His special work. Then He meditates, and forms—as thoughts—come forth. There His manifest work may be said to end, though He maintains ever the life of the atom. As far as the active work of the kosmos is concerned, He gives way to the next of the great forces that is to work, the force of Vişhņu. His work is to gather together that matter that has been built, shaped, prepared, vivified, and build it into definite forms after the creative ideas brought forth by the meditation of Brahmâ. He gives to matter a binding force; He gives to it those energies that hold form together. No form exists without Him, whether it be moving or unmoving. How often does Shrî Kṛişhņa, speaking as the supreme Vişhņu, lay stress on this fact. He is the life in every form; without it the form could not exist, without it it would go back to its primeval elements and no longer live as form. He is the all-pervading life; the "Supporter of the Universe" is one of His names. Mahâdeva has a different function in the universe; especially is He the great Yogî; especially is He the great Teacher, the Mahâguru; He is sometimes called Jagatguru, the Teacher of the world. Over and over again—to take a comparatively modern example, as the *Gurugîtâ*—we find Him as Teacher, to whom Pârvati goes asking for instruction as to the nature of the Guru. He it is who defines the Guru's work, He it is who inspires the Guru's teaching. Every Guru on earth is a reflection of Mahâdeva, and it is His life which he is commissioned to give out to the world. Yogî, immersed in contemplation, taking the ascetic form always—that marks out His functions. For the symbols by which the mighty Ones are shown in the teachings are not meaningless, but are replete with the deepest meaning. And when you see Him represented as the eternal Yogî, with the cord in His hand, sitting as an ascetic in contemplation, it means that He is the supreme ideal of the ascetic life, and that men who come especially under His influence must pass out of home, out of family, out of the normal ties of evolution, and give themselves to a life of asceticism, to a life of renunciation, to share, however feebly, in that mighty yoga by which the universe is kept alive.

He then manifests not as Avatâra, but such manifestations come from Him who is the God, the Spirit, of evolution, who evolves all forms. That is why from Vişhņu all these Avatâras come. For it is He who by His infinite love dwells in every form that He has made; with patience that nothing can exhaust, with love that nothing can tire, with quiet, calm endurance which no folly of man can shake from its eternal peace, He lives in every form, moulding it as it will bear the moulding, shaping it as it yields itself to His impulse, binding Himself, limiting Himself in order that His universe may grow, Lord of eternal life and bliss, dwelling in every form. If you grasp this, it is not difficult to say why from Him alone the Avatâras come. Who else should take form save the One who gives form? who else should work with this unending love save He, who, while the universe exists, binds Himself that the universe may live and ultimately share His freedom? He is bound that the universe may be free. Who else then should come forth when special need arises?

And He gives the great types. Let me remind you of the *Shrîmad-Bhâgavata*, where in an early chapter of the first Book, the 3rd chapter, a very long list is given of the forms that Vişhņu took, not only the great Avatâras, but also a large number of others. It is said He appeared as Nara and Nârâyana; it is said He appeared as Kapila; He took female forms, and so on, a whole long list being given of the shapes that He assumed. And, turning from that to a very illuminative passage in the *Mahâbhârata*, we find Him in the form of Shrî Kṛişhņa explaining a profound truth to Arjuna.

There He gives the law of these appearances: "When, O son of Pritha, I live in the order of the deities, then I act in every respect as a deity. When I live in the order of the Gandharvas, then I act in every respect as a Gandharva. When I live in the order of the Nâgas, I act as a Nâga. When I live in the order of the Yakshas, or that of the Râkshasas, I act after the manner of that order. Born now in the order of humanity, I must act as a human being." A profound truth, a truth that few in modern times recognise. Every type in the universe, in its own place, is good; every type in the universe, in its own place, is necessary. There is no life save His life; how then could any type come into existence apart from the universal life, bereft whereof nothing can exist?

We speak of good forms and evil, and rightly, as regards our own evolution. But from the wider standpoint of the kosmos, good and evil are relative terms, and everything is very good in the sight of the Supreme who lives in every one. How can a type come into existence in which He cannot live? How can anything live and move, save as it has its being in Him? Each type has its work; each type has its place; the type of the Râkshasa as much as the type of the Deva, of the Asura as much as of the Sura. Let me give you one curious little simple example, which yet has a certain graphic force. You have a pole you want to move, and that pole is on a pivot, like the mountain which churned the ocean, a pole with its two ends, positive and negative we will call them. The positive end, we will say, is pushed in the direction of the river (the river flowing beyond one end of the hall at Adyar). The negative pole is pushed—in what direction? In the opposite. And those who are pushing it have their faces turned in the opposite direction. One man looks at the river, the other man has his back to it, looking in the opposite direction. But the pole turns in the one direction although they push in opposite directions. They are working round the same circle, and the pole goes faster because it is pushed from its two ends. There is the picture of our universe. The positive force you call the Deva or Sura; his face is turned, it seems, to God. The negative force you call the Râkshasa or Asura; his face, it seems, is turned away from God. Ah no! God is everywhere, in every point of the circle round which they tread; and they tread His circle and do His will and no otherwise; and all at length find rest and peace in Him.

Therefore Shrî Kṛiṣhṇa Himself can incarnate in the form of Râkshasa, and when in that form He will act as Râkshasa and not as Deva, doing that part of the divine work with the same perfection as He does the other, which men in their limited vision call the good. A great truth hard to grasp. I shall have to return to it presently in speaking of Râvana, one of the mightiest types of, perhaps the greatest of, all the Râkshasas. And we shall see, if we can follow, how the profound truth works out. But remember, if in the minds of some of you there is some hesitation in accepting this, that the words that I read are not mine, but those of the Lord who spoke of His own embodying; He has left on record for your teaching, that He has embodied Himself in the form of Râkshasa and has acted after the manner of that order.

Leaving that for a moment, there is one other point I must take, ere speaking of the need for Avatâras, and it is this: when the great central Deities have manifested, then there come forth from Them seven Deities of what we may call the second order. In Theosophy, they are spoken of as the planetary Logoi, to distinguish them from the great solar Logoi, the central Life. Each of These has to do with one of the seven sacred planets, and with the chain of worlds connected with that planet. Our world is one of the links in this chain, and you and I pass round this chain in successive incarnations in the great stages of life. The world—our present world—is the midway globe of one such chain. One Logos of the secondary order presides over the evolution of this chain of worlds. He shows out three aspects, reflections of the great Logoi who are at the centre of the system. You have read perhaps of the seven-leaved lotus, the Saptaparnapadma; looked at with the higher sight, gazed at with the open vision of the seer, that mighty group of creative and directing Beings looks like the lotus with its seven leaves and the great Ones are at the heart of the lotus. It is as though you could see a vast lotus-flower spread out in space, the tips of the seven leaves being the mighty Intelligences presiding over the evolution of the chains of worlds. That lotus symbol is no mere symbol but a high reality, as seen in that wondrous world wherefrom the symbol has been taken by the sages. And because the great Ṛishis of old saw with the open eye of knowledge, saw the lotus-flower spread in space, they took it as the symbol of kosmos, the lotus with its seven leaves, each one a mighty Deva presiding over a separate line of evolution. We are primarily concerned with our own planetary Deva and through Him with the great Devas of the solar system.

Now my reason for mentioning this is to explain one word that has puzzled many students. Mahâvishṇu, the great Vishṇu, why that particular epithet? What does it mean when that phrase is used? It means the great solar Logos, Vishṇu in His essential nature: but there is a reflection of His glory, a reflection of His power, of His love, in more immediate connection with ourselves and our own world. He is His representative, as a viceroy may represent the king. Some of the Avatâras we shall find came forth from Mahâvishṇu through the planetary Logos, who is concerned with our evolution and the evolution of the world. But the Pûrṇâvatâra that I spoke of yesterday comes forth directly from Mahâvishṇu, with no intermediary between Himself and the world that He comes to help. Here is another distinction between the Pûrṇâvatâra and those more limited ones, that I could not mention yesterday, because the words used would, at that stage, have been unintelligible. We shall find to-morrow, when we come to deal with the Avatâras Matsya, Kûrma, and so on, that these special Avatâras, connected with the evolution of certain types in the world, while indirectly from Mahâvishṇu, come through the mediation of His mighty representative for our own chain, the wondrous Intelligence that conveys His love and ministers His will, and is the channel of His all-pervading and supporting power. When we come to study Shrî Kṛishṇa we shall find that there is no intermediary. He stands as the Supreme Himself. And while in the other cases there is the Presence that may be recognised as an intermediary, it is absent in the case of the great Lord of Life.

Leaving that for further elaboration then to-morrow, let us try to answer the next question, "How arises this need for Avatâras?" because in the minds of some, quite naturally, a difficulty does arise. The difficulty that many thoughtful people feel may be formulated thus: "Surely the whole plan of the world is in the mind of the Logos from the beginning, and surely we cannot suppose that He is working like a human workman, not thoroughly understanding that at which He aims. He must be the architect as well as the builder; He must make the plan as well as carry it out. He is not like the mason who puts a stone in the wall where he is told, and knows nothing of the architecture of the building to which he is contributing. He is the master-builder, the great architect of the universe, and everything in the plan of that universe must be in His mind ere ever the universe began. But if that be so—and we cannot think otherwise—how is it that the need for special intervention arises? Does not the fact of special intervention imply some unforeseen difficulty that has arisen? If there must be a kind of interference with the working out of the plan, does that not look as if in the original plan some force was left out of account, some difficulty had not been seen, something had arisen for which preparation had not been made? If it be not so, why the need for interference, which looks as though it were brought about to meet an unforeseen event?" A natural, reasonable, and perfectly fair question. Let us try to answer it. I do not believe in shirking difficulties; it is better to look them in the face, and see if an answer be possible.

Now the answer comes along three different lines. There are three great classes of facts, each of which contributes to the necessity; and each, foreseen by the Logos, is definitely prepared for as needing a particular manifestation.

The first of these lines arises from what I may perhaps call the nature of things. I remarked at the beginning of this lecture on the fact that our universe, our system, is part of a greater whole, not separate, not independent, not primary, in comparatively a low scale in the universe, our sun a planet in a vaster system. Now what does that imply? As regards matter, Prakṛiti, it implies that our system is builded out of matter already existing, out of matter already gifted with certain properties, out of matter that spreads through all space, and from which every Logos takes His materials, modifying it according to His own plan and according to His own will. When we speak of Mûlaprakṛiti, the root of matter, we do not mean that it exists as the matter we know. No philosopher, no thinker would dream of saying that that which spreads throughout space is identical with the matter of our very elementary solar system. It is the root of matter, that of which all forms of matter are merely modifications. What does that imply? It implies that our great Lord, who brought our solar system into existence, is taking matter which already has certain properties given to it by One yet mightier than Himself. In that matter three guṇas exist in equilibrium, and it is the breath of the Logos that throws them out of equilibrium, and causes the motion by which our system is brought into existence. There must be a throwing out of equilibrium, for equilibrium means Pralaya, where there is not motion, nor any manifestation of life and form. When life and form come forth, equilibrium must have been disturbed, and motion must be liberated by which the world shall be built. But the moment you grasp that truth you see that there must be certain limitations by virtue of the very material in which the Deity is working for the making of the system. It is true that when out of His system, when not conditioned and confined and limited by it, as He is by His most gracious will, it is true that He would be the Lord of that matter by virtue of His union with the mightier Life beyond; but when for the building of the world He limits Himself within His Mâyâ, then He must work within the conditions of those materials that limit His activity, as we are told over and over again.

Now when in the ceaseless interplay of Sattva, Rajas, and Tamas, Tamas has the ascendancy, aided and, as it were, worked by Rajas, so that they predominate over Sattva in the foreseen evolution, when the two combining overpower the third, when the force of Rajas and the inertia and stubbornness of Tamas, binding themselves together, check the action, the harmony, the pleasure-giving qualities of Sattva, then comes one of the conditions in which the Lord comes forth to restore that which had been disturbed of the balanced interworking of the three guṇas and to make again such balance between them as shall enable evolution to go forward smoothly and not be checked in its progress. He re-establishes the balance of power which gives orderly motion, the order having been disturbed by the co-operation of the two in contradistinction to the third. In these fundamental attributes of matter, the three guṇas, lies the first reason of the need for Avatâras.

The second need has to do with man himself, and now we come back in both the second and the third to that question of good and evil, of which I have already spoken. I´shvara, when He came to deal with the evolution of man—with all reverence I say it—had a harder task to perform than in the evolution of the lower forms of life. On them the law is imposed and they must obey its impulse. On the mineral the law is compulsory; every mineral moves according to the law, without interposing any impulse from itself to work against the will of the One. In the vegetable world the law is imposed, and every plant grows in orderly method according to the law within it, developing steadily and in the fashion of its order, interposing no impulse of its own. Nay, in the animal world—save perhaps when we come to its highest members—the law is still a force overpowering everything else, sweeping everything before it, carrying along all living things. A wheel turning on the road might carry with it on its axle the fly that happened to have settled there; it does not interpose any obstacle to the turning of the wheel. If the fly comes on to the circumference of the wheel and opposes itself to its motion, it is crushed without the slightest jarring of the wheel that rolls on, and the form goes out of existence, and the life takes other shapes.

So is the wheel of law in the three lower kingdoms. But with man it is not so. In man I´shvara sets himself to produce an image of Himself, which is not the case in the lower kingdoms. As life has evolved, one force after another has come out, and in man there begins to come out the central life, for the time has arrived for the evolution of the sovereign power of will, the self-initiated motion which is part of the life of the Supreme. Do not misunderstand me—for the subject is a subtle one; there is only one will in the universe, the will of I´shvara, and all must conform itself to that will, all is conditioned by that will, all must move according to that will, and that will marks out the straight line of evolution. There may be swerving neither to the right hand nor to the left. There is one will only which in its aspect to us is free, but inasmuch as our life is the life of I´shvara Himself, inasmuch as there is but one Self and that Self is yours and mine as much as His—for He has given us His very Self to be our Self and our life—there must evolve at one stage of this wondrous evolution that royal power of will which is seen in Him. And from the A´tmâ within us, which is Himself in us, there flows forth the sovereign will into the sheaths in which the A´tmâ is as it were held. Now what happens is this: force goes out through the sheaths and gives them some of its own nature, and each sheath begins to set up a reflection of the will on its own account, and you get the "I" of the body which wants to go this way, and the "I" of passion or emotion which wants to go that way, and the "I" of the mind which wants to go a third way, and none of these ways is the way of the A´tmâ, the Supreme. These are the illusory wills of man, and there is one way in which you may distinguish them from the true will. Each of them is determined in its direction by external attraction; the man's body wants to move in a particular way because something attracts it, or something else repels it: it moves to what it likes, to what is congenial to it, it moves away from that which it dislikes, from that from which it feels itself repelled. But that motion of the body is but motion determined by the I´shvara outside, as it were, rather than by the I´shvara within, by the kosmos around and not by the Self within, which has not yet achieved its mastery of the kosmos. So with the emotions or passions: they are drawn this way or that by the objects of the senses, and the "senses move after their appropriate objects"; it is not the "I," the Self, which moves. And so also with the mind. "The mind is fickle and restless, O Kṛiṣhṇa, it seems as hard to curb as the wind," and the mind lets the senses run after objects as a horse that has broken its reins flies away with the unskilled driver. All these forces are set up; and there is one more thing to remember. These forces reinforce the râjasic guṇa and help to bring about that predominance of which I spoke; all these reckless desires that are not according to the one will are yet necessary in order that the will may evolve and in order to train and develop the man.

Do you say why? How would you learn right if you knew not wrong? How would you choose good if you knew not evil? How would you recognise the light if there were no darkness? How would you move if there were no resistance? The forces that are called dark, the forces of the Râkshasas, of the Asuras, of all that seem to be working against I´shvara—these are the forces that call out the inner strength of the Self in man, by struggling with which the forces of A´tmâ within the man are developed, and without which he would remain in Pralaya for evermore. It is a perfectly stagnant pool where there is no motion, and there you get corruption and not life. The evolution of force can only be made by struggle, by combat, by effort, by exercise, and inasmuch as I´shvara is building men and not babies, He must draw out men's forces by pulling against their strength, making them struggle in order to attain, and so vivifying into outer manifestation the life that otherwise would remain enfolded in itself. In the seed the life is hidden, but it will not grow if you leave the seed alone. Place it on this table here, and come back a century hence, and, if you find it, it will be a seed still and nothing more. So also is the A´tmâ in man ere evolution and struggle have begun. Plant your seed in the ground, so that the forces in the ground press on it, and the rays of the sun from outside make vibrations that work on it, and the water from the rain comes through the soil into it and forces it to swell—then the seed begins to grow; but as it begins to grow it finds the earth around. How shall it grow but by pushing at it and so bringing out the energies of life that are within it? And against the opposition of the ground the roots strike down, and against the opposition of the ground the growing point mounts upward, and by the opposition of the ground the forces are evolved that make the seed grow, and the little plant appears above the soil. Then the wind comes and blows and tries to drag it away, and, in order that it may live and not perish, it strikes its roots deeper and gives itself a better hold against the battering force of the wind, and so the tree grows against the forces which try to tear it out. And if these forces were not, there would have been no growth of the root. And so with the root of I'shvara, the life within us; were everything around us smooth and easy, we would remain supine, lethargic, indifferent. It is the whip of pain, of suffering, of disappointment, that drives us onward and brings out the forces of our internal life which otherwise would remain undeveloped. Would you have a man grow? Then don't throw him on a couch with pillows on every side, and bring his meals and put them into his mouth, so that he moves not limb nor exercises mind. Throw him on a desert, where there is no food nor water to be found; let the sun beat down on his head, the wind blow against him; let his mind be made to think how to meet the necessities of the body, and the man grows into a man and not a log. That is why there are forces which you call evil. In this universe there is no evil; all is good that comes to us from I′shvara, but it sometimes comes in the guise of evil that, by opposing it, we may draw out our strength. Then we begin to understand that these forces are necessary, and that they are within the plan of I′shvara. They test evolution, they strengthen evolution, so that it does not take the next step onward till it has strength enough to hold its own, one step made firm by opposition before the next is taken. But when, by the conflicting wills of men, the forces that work for retardation, to keep a man back till he is able to overcome them and go on, when they are so reinforced by men's unruly wishes that they are beginning, as it were, to threaten progress, then ere that check takes place, there is reinforcement from the other side: the presence of the Avatâra of the forces that threaten evolution calls forth the presence of the Avatâra that leads to the progress of humanity.

We come to the third cause. The Avatâra does not come forth without a call. The earth, it is said, is very heavy with its load of evil, "Save us, O supreme Lord," the Devas come and cry. In answer to that cry the Lord comes forth. But what is this that I spoke of purposely by a strange phrase to catch your attention, that I spoke of as an Avatâra of evil? By the will of the one Supreme, there is one incarnated in form who gathers up together the forces that make for retardation, in order that, thus gathered together, they may be destroyed by the opposing force of good, and thus the balance may be re-established and evolution go on along its appointed road. Devas work for joy, the reward of Heaven. Svarga is their home, and they serve the Supreme for the joys that there they have. Râkshasas also serve Him, first for rule on earth, and power to grasp and hold and enjoy as they will in this lower world. Both sides serve for reward, and are moved by the things that please.

And in order, as our time is drawing to a close, that I may take one great example to show how these work, let me take the mighty one, Râvana of Lanka,[1] that we may give a concrete form to a rather difficult and abstruse thought. Râvana, as you all know, was the mighty intelligence, the Râkshasa, who called forth the coming of Shrî Râma. But look back into the past, and what was he? Keeper of Viṣhṇu's heaven, door-keeper of the mighty Lord, devotee, bhakta, absolutely devoted to the Lord. Look at his past, and where do you find a bhakta of Mahâdeva more absolute in devotion than the one who came forth later as Râvana? It was he who cast his head into the fire in order that Mahâdeva might be served. It is he in whose name have been written some of the most exquisite stotras, breathing the spirit of completest devotion; in one of them, you may remember—and you could scarcely carry devotion to a further point—it is in the mouth of Râvana words are put appealing to Mahâdeva, and describing Him as surrounded by forms the most repellent and undesirable, surrounded on every side by pisâchas and bhûtas,[2] which to us seem but the embodiment of the dark

[1] Ceylon.
[2] Goblins and elementals.

shadows of the burning ghat, forms from which all beauty is withdrawn. He cries out in a passion of love:

Better wear pisâcha-form, so we
Evermore are near and wait on Thee.

How did he then come to be the ravisher of Sîtâ and the enemy of God?

You know how through lack of intuition, through lack of power to recognise the meaning of an order, following the words not the spirit, following the outside not the inner, he refused to open the door of heaven when Sanat Kumâra came and demanded entrance. In order that that which was lacking might be filled, in order that that which was wanting might be earned, that which was called a curse was pronounced, a curse which was the natural reaction from the mistake. He was asked: "Will you have seven incarnations friendly to Viṣhṇu, or three in which you will be His enemy and oppose Him?" And because he was a true bhakta, and because every moment of absence from his Lord meant to him hell of torture, he chose three of enmity, which would let him go back sooner to the Feet of the Beloved, rather than the seven of happiness, of friendliness. Better a short time of utter enmity than a longer remaining away with apparent happiness. It was love not hatred that made him choose the form of a Râkshasa rather than the form of a Ṛishi. There is the first note of explanation.

Then, coming into the form of Râkshasa, he must do his duty as Râkshasa. This was no weak man to be swayed by momentary thought, by transient objects. He had all the learning of the Vedas. With him, it was said, passed away Vaidic learning, with him it disappeared from earth. He knew his duty. What was his duty? To put forward every force which was in his mighty nature in order to check evolution, and so call out every force in man which could be called out by opposing energy which had to be overcome; to gather round him all the forces which were opposing evolution; to make himself king of the whole, centre and law-giver to every force that was setting itself against the will of the Lord; to gather them together as it were into one head, to call them together into one arm; so that when their apparent triumph made the cry of the earth go up to Viṣhṇu, the answer might come in Râma's Avatâra and they be destroyed, that the life-wave might go on.

Nobly he did the work, thoroughly he discharged his duty. It is said that even sages are confused about Dharma, and truly it is subtle and hard to grasp in its entirety, though the fragment the plain man sees be simple enough. His Dharma was the Dharma of a Râkshasa, to lead the whole forces of evil against One whom in his inner soul, then clouded, he loved. When Shrî Râma came, when He was wandering in the forest, how could he sting Him into leaving the life of His life, His beloved Sîtâ, and into coming out into the world to do His work? By taking away from Him the one thing to which He clung, by taking away from Him the wife whom He loved as His very Self, by placing her in the spot where all the forces of evil were gathered together, so making one head for destruction, which the arrow of Shrî Râma might destroy. Then the mighty battle, then the struggle with all the forces of his great nature, that the law might be obeyed to the uttermost, duly fulfilled to the last grain, the debt paid that was owed; and then—ah then! the shaft of the Beloved, then the arrow of Shrî Râma that struck off the head from the seeming enemy, from the real devotee. And from the corpse of the Râkshasa that fell upon the field near Lanka, the devotee went up to Goloka[1] to sit at the feet of the Beloved, and rest for awhile till the third incarnation had to be lived out.

Such then are some of the reasons by, the ways in which the coming of the Avatâra is brought about. And my last word to you, my brothers, to-day is but a sentence, in order to avoid the possibility of a mistake to which our diving into these depths of thought may possibly give rise. Remember that though all powers are His, all forces His, Râkshasa as much as Deva, Asura as much as Sura; remember that for your evolution you must be on the side of good, and struggle to the utmost against evil. Do not let the thoughts I have put lead you into a bog, into a pit of hell, in which you may for the time perish, that because evil is relative, because it exists by the one will, because Râkshasa is His as much as Deva, therefore you shall go on their side and walk along their path. It is not so. If you yield to ambition, if you yield to pride, if you set yourselves against the will of I´shvara, if you struggle for the separated self, if in yourselves now you identify yourself with the past in which you have dwelt instead of with the future towards which you should be directing your steps, then, if your Karma be at a certain stage, you pass into the ranks of those who work as enemies, because you have chosen that fate for yourself, at the promptings of the lower nature. Then with bitter inner pain—even if with complete submission—accepting the Karma, but with profound sorrow, you shall have to work out your own will against the will of the Beloved, and feel the anguish of the rending that separates the inner from the outer life. The will of I´shvara for you is evolution; these forces are made to help your evolution—*but only if you strive against them*. If you yield to them, then they carry you away. You do not then call out your own strength, but only strengthen them. Therefore, O Arjuna, stand up and fight. Do not be supine; do not yield yourself to the forces; they are there to call out your energies by opposition and you must not sink down on the floor of the chariot. And my last word is the word of Shrî Kṛiṣhṇa to Arjuna: "Take up your bow, stand up and fight."

[1] A name for one of the heavens.

THIRD LECTURE.

Some Special Avatâras

THE subject this morning, my brothers, is in some ways an easy and in other ways a difficult one; easy, inasmuch as the stories of the Avatâras can be readily told and readily grasped; difficult, inasmuch as the meaning that underlies these manifestations may possibly be in some ways unfamiliar, may not have been thoroughly thought out by individual hearers. And I must begin with a general word as to these special Avatâras. You may remember that I said that the whole universe may be regarded as the Avatâra of the Supreme, the Self-revelation of I′shvara. But we are not dealing with that general Self-revelation; nor are we even considering the very many revelations that have taken place from time to time, marked out by special characteristics; for we have seen by referring to one or two of the old writings that many lists are given of the comings of the Lord, and we are to-day concerned with only some of those, those that are accepted specially as Avatâras.

Now on one point I confess myself puzzled at the outset, and I do not know whether in your exoteric literature light is thrown upon the point as to how these ten were singled out, who was the person who chose them out of a longer list, on what authority that list was proclaimed. On that point I must simply state the question, leaving it unanswered. It may be a matter familiar to those who have made researches into the exoteric literature. It is not a point of quite sufficient importance for the moment to spend on it time and trouble, in what we may call the occult way of research. I leave that then aside, for there is one reason why some of these stand out in a way which is clear and definite. They mark stages in the evolution of the world. They mark new departures in the growth of the developing life, and whether it was that fact which underlay the exoteric choice I am unable to say; but certainly that fact by itself is sufficient to justify the special distinction which is made.

There is one other general point to consider. Accounts of these Avatâras are found in the Purâṇas; allusions to them, to one or other of them, are found in other of the ancient writings, but the moment you come to very much detail you must turn to the Paurâṇic accounts; as you are aware, sages, in giving those Purâṇas, very often described things as they are seen on the higher planes, giving the description of the underlying truth of facts and events; you have appearances described which sound very strange in the lower world; you have facts asserted which raise very much of challenge in modern days. When you read in the Purâṇas of strange forms and marvellous appearances, when you read accounts of creatures that seem unlike anything that you have ever heard of or dreamed of elsewhere, the modern mind, with its somewhat narrow limitations, is apt to revolt against the accounts that are given; the modern mind, trained within the limits of the science of observation, is necessarily circumscribed within those limits and those limits are of an exceedingly narrow description; they are limits which belong only to modern time, modern to men, in the true sense of the word, though geological researches stretch of course far back into what we call in this nineteenth century the night of time. But you must remember that the moment geology goes beyond the historic period, which is a mere moment in the history of the world, it has more of guesses than of facts, more of theories than of proofs. If you take half a dozen modern geologists and ask each of them in turn for the date of the period of which records remain in the small number of fossils collected, you will find that almost every man gives a different date, and that they deal with differences of millions of years as though they were only seconds or minutes of ours. So that you will have to remember in what science can tell you of the world, however accurate it may be within its limits, that these limits are exceedingly narrow, narrow I mean when measured by the sight that goes back kalpa after kalpa, and that knows that the mind of the Supreme is not limited to the manifestations of a few hundred thousands of years, but goes back million after million, hundreds of millions after hundreds of millions, and that the varieties of form, the enormous differences of types, the marvellous kinds of creatures which have come out of that creative imagination, transcend in actuality all that man's mind can dream of, and that the very wildest images that man can make fail far short of the realities that actually existed in the past kalpas through which the universe has gone. That word of warning is necessary, and also the warning that on the higher planes things look very different from what they look down here. You have here a reflection only of part of those higher forms of existence. Space there has more dimensions than it has on the physical plane, and each dimension of space adds a new fundamental variety to form; if to illustrate this I may use a simile I have often used, it may perhaps convey to you a little idea of what I mean. Two similes I will take each throwing a little light on a very difficult subject. Suppose that a picture is presented to you of a solid form; the picture, being made by pen or pencil on a sheet of paper, must show on the sheet, which is practically of two dimensions—a plane surface—a three dimensional form; so that if you want to represent a solid object, a vase, you must draw it flat, and you can only represent the solidity of that vase by resorting to certain devices of light and shade, to the artificial device which is called perspective, in order to make an illusory semblance of the third dimension. There on the plane surface you get a solid appearance, and the eye is deceived into thinking it sees a solid when really it is looking at a flat surface. Now as a matter of fact if you show a picture to a savage, an undeveloped savage, or to a very young child, they will not see a solid but only a flat. They will not recognise the picture as being the picture of a solid object they have seen in the world round them; they will not see that that artificial representation is meant to show a familiar solid, and it passes by them without making any impression on the mind; only the education of the eye enables you to see on a flat surface the picture of a solid form. Now, by an effort of the imagination, can you think of a solid as being the representation of a form in one dimension more, shown by a kind of perspective? Then you may get a vague idea of what is meant when we speak of a further dimension in space. As the picture is to the vase, so is the vase to a higher object of which that vase itself is a reflection. So again if you think, say, of the lotus flower I spoke of yesterday, as having just the tips of its leaves above water, each tip would appear as a separate object. If you know the whole you know that they are all parts of one object; but coming over the surface of the water you will see tips only, one for each leaf of the seven-leaved lotus. So is every globe in space an apparently separate object, while in reality it is not separated at all, but part of a whole that exists in a space of more dimensions; and the separateness is mere illusion due to the limitations of our faculties.

Now I have made this introduction in order to show you that when you read the

Purâṇas you consistently get the fact on the higher plane described in terms of the lower, with the result that it seems unintelligible, seems incomprehensible; then you have what is called an allegory, that is, a reality which looks like a fancy down here, but is a deeper truth than the illusion of physical matter, and is nearer to the reality of things than the things which you call objective and real. If you follow that line of thought at all you will read the Purâṇas with more intelligence and certainly with more reverence than some of the modern Hindus are apt to show in the reading, and you will begin to understand that when another vision is opened one sees things differently from the way that one sees them on the physical plane, and that that which seems impossible on the physical is what is really seen when you pass beyond the physical limitations.

From the Purâṇas then the stories come.

Let me take the first three Avatâras apart from the remainder, for a reason that you will readily understand as we go through them. We take the Avatâra which is spoken of as that of Matsya or the fish; that which is spoken of as that of Kûrma or the tortoise; that which is spoken of as that of Vârâha, or the boar. Three animal forms; how strange! thinks the modern graduate. How strange that the Supreme should take the forms of these lower animals, a fish, a tortoise, a boar! What childish folly! "The babbling of a race in its infancy," it is said by the pandits of the Western world. Do not be so sure. Why this wonderful conceit as to the human form? Why should you and I be the only worthy vessels of the Deity that have come out of the illimitable Mind in the course of ages? What is there in this particular shape of head, arms, and trunk which shall make it the only worthy vessel to serve as a manifestation of the supreme I′shvara? I know of nothing so wonderful in the mere outer form that should make that shape alone worthy to represent some of the aspects of the Highest. And may it not be that from His standpoint those great differences that we see between ourselves and those which we call the lower forms of life may be almost imperceptible, since He transcends them all? A little child sees an immense difference between himself of perhaps two and a half feet high and a baby only a foot and a half high, and thinks himself a man compared with that tiny form rolling on the ground and unable to walk. But to the grown man there is not so much difference between the length of the two, and one seems very much like the other. While we are very small we see great differences between ourselves and others; but on the mountain top the hovel and the palace do not differ so very much in height. They all look like ant-hills, very much of the same size. And so from the standpoint of I′shvara, in the vast hierarchies from the mineral to the loftiest Deva, the distinctions are but as ant-hills in comparison with Himself, and one form or another is equally worthy, so that it suits His purpose, and manifests His will.

Now for the Matsya Avatâra; the story you will all know: when the great Manu, Vaivasvata Manu, the Root Manu, as we call Him—that is, a Manu not of one race only, but of a whole vast round of kosmic evolution, presiding over the seven globes that are linked for the evolution of the world—that mighty Manu, sitting one day immersed in contemplation, sees a tiny fish gasping for water; and moved by compassion, as all great ones are, He takes up the little fish and puts it in a bowl, and the fish grows till it fills the bowl; and He placed it in a water vessel and it grew to the size of the vessel; then He took it out of that vessel and put it into a bigger one; afterwards into a tank, a pond, a river, the sea, and still the marvellous fish grew and grew and grew. The time came when a vast change was impending; one of those changes called a minor pralaya, and it was necessary that the seeds of life should be carried over that pralaya to the next manvantara. That would be a minor pralaya and a minor manvantara. What does that mean? It means a passage of the seeds of life from one globe to another; from what a we call the globe preceding our own to our own earth. It is the function of the Root Manu, with the help and the guidance of the planetary Logos, to transfer the seeds of life from one globe to the next, so as to plant them in a new soil where further growth is possible. As waters rose, waters of matter submerging the globe which was passing into pralaya, an ark, a vessel appeared; into this vessel stepped the great Ṛishi with others, and the seeds of life were carried by Them, and as They go forth upon the waters a mighty fish appears and to the horn of that fish the vessel is fastened by a rope, and it conveys the whole safely to the solid ground where the Manu rebegins His work. A story! yes, but a story that tells a truth; for looking at it as it takes place in the history of the world, we see the vast surging ocean of matter, we see the Root Manu and the great Initiates with Him gathering up the seeds of life from the world whose work is over, carrying them under the guidance and with the help of the planetary Viṣhṇu to the new globe where new impulse is to be given to the life; and the reason why the fish form was chosen was simply because in the building up again of the world, it was at first covered with water, and only that form of life was originally possible, so far as denser physical life was concerned.

You have in that first stage what the geologists call the Silurian Age, the age of fishes, when the great divine manifestation was of all these forms of life. The Purâṇa rightly starts in the previous Kalpa, rightly starts the manifestations with the manifestation in the form of the fish. Not so very ridiculous after all, you see, when read by knowledge instead of by ignorance; a truth, as the Purâṇas are full of truth, if they were only read with intelligence and not with prejudice.

But some of you may say that there is confusion about these first Avatâras; in several accounts we find that the Boar stands the first; that is true, but the key of it is this; the Boar Avatâra initiated that evolution which was followed unbrokenly by the human; whereas the other two bring in great stages, each of which is regarded as a separate kalpa; and if you look into the *Viṣhṇu Purâṇa* you will find there the key; for when that begins to relate the incarnation of the Boar, there is just a sentence thrown in, that the Matsya and Kûrma Avatâras belong to previous kalpas.

Now if we take the theosophical nomenclature, we find each of these kalpas covers what we call a Root Race, and you may remember that the first Root Race of humanity had not human form at all but was simply a floating mass able to live in the waters which then covered the earth, and only showing the ordinary protoplasmic motions connected with such a type of life and possible at that stage of its evolution. It was a seed of form rather than a form itself; it was the seed planted by the Manu in the waters of the earth, that out of that humanity might evolve. But the general course of physical evolution passed through the stage of the fish; and geology there gives a true fact, though it does not understand, naturally, the hidden meaning; while the Purâṇa gives you the reality of the manifestation, and the deeper truth that underlies the stages of the evolving world.

Then we find, tracing it onward, that this great age passes, and the world begins to rise out of the waters. How then shall types be brought forth in order that evolution may go on? The next great type is to be fitted either for land or for water; for the next stage of the earth shows the waters draining gradually away, and the land appearing, and the creatures that are the marked characteristic of the age must exist partially on land and partially in water. Here again there must be manifestation of the type of life, this time of what we call the reptile type; the tortoise is chosen as the typical creature, and while the tortoise typifies the type to be evolved, reptiles, amphibious creatures of every description, swarm over the earth, becoming more and more land-like in their character as the proportion of land to water increases. There is meanwhile going on, in the "imperishable sacred land," a preparation for further evolution. There is one part of the globe that changes not, that from the beginning has been, and will last while the globe is lasting; it is called the "imperishable land." And there the great Ṛishis gather, and thence they ever come forth for the helping of man; that is the imperishable sacred land, sometimes called the "sacred pole of the earth." Pole itself exists not on the physical plane but on the higher, and its reflection coming downward makes, as it were, one spot which never changes, but is ever guarded from the tread of ordinary men. There took place a most instructive phenomenon. The type of the evolution then preceding, the Tortoise, the Logos in that form, makes Himself the base of the revolving axis of evolution. That is typified by Mandâra, the mountain which, placed on the tortoise, is made to revolve by the hosts of Suras and Asuras, one pulling at the head of the serpent, and the other at the tail—the positive and negative forces that I spoke of yesterday. So the churning begins in matter, evolving types of life. The type is ever evolved before the lower manifestation, the type appears before the copies of it are born in the lower world. And how often have the students of the great Teachers themselves seen the very thing occur; the churning of the waters of matter giving forth all the types of the many sorts and species that are generated in the lower world; these are the archetypes, as we call them, of classes and creatures, always produced in preparation for the forward stretch of evolution. There came forth one by one the archetypes, the elephant, the horse, the woman, and so on, one after another, showing the track along which evolution was to go. And first of all, Amṛita, nectar of immortality, comes forth, symbol of the one life which passes through every form—and that life appears above the waters the taking of which is necessary in order that every form may live.

We cannot delay on details; I can only trace hastily the outline, showing you how real is the truth that underlies the story, and as that gradually goes on and the types are ready, there comes the whelming of the world under the waters, and the great continents vanish for a time.

Then comes the third Avatâra, the Vârâha. No earth is to be seen; the waters of the flood have overwhelmed it. The types that are to be produced on earth are waiting in the higher region for place on which to manifest. How shall the earth be brought up from the waters which have overwhelmed it? Now once again the great Helper is needed, the God, the Protector of Evolution. Then in the form of a mighty Boar, whose form filled the heaven, plunging down into the waters that He alone could separate, the Great One descends. He brings up the earth from the lower region where it was lying awaiting His coming; and the land rises up again from below the surface of the flood, and the vast Lemurian continent is the earth of that far-off age. Here science has a word to say, rightly enough, that on the Lemurian continent were developed many types of life, and there the mammals first made their appearance. Quite so; that was exactly what the sages taught thousands upon thousands of years ago; that when the Boar, the great type of the mammal, plunged into the waters to bring up the earth, then was started the mammalian evolution, and the continent thus rescued from the waters was crowded with the forms of the mammalian kingdom. Just as the Fish had typified the Silurian epoch, just as the Tortoise had started on its way the great amphibian evolution, so did the Boar, that typical mammal, start the mammalian evolution, and we come to the Lemurian continent with its wonderful variety of forms of mammalian life. Not so very ignorant after all, you see, the ancient writings! For men are only re-discovering to-day what has been in the hands of the followers of the Ṛishis for thousands, tens of thousands of years.

Then we come to a strange incarnation on this Lemurian continent: frightful conflicts existed; we are nearing what in the theosophical nomenclature is the middle of the third Race, and man as man will shortly appear with all the characteristics of his nature. He is not yet quite come to birth; strange forms are seen, half human and half animal, wholly monstrous; terrible struggles arise between these monstrous forms born from the slime as it is said—from the remains of former creations—and the newer and higher life in which the future evolution is enshrined. These forms are represented in the Purâṇas as those of the race of Daityas, who ruled the earth, who struggled against the Deva manifestations, who conquered the Devas from time to time, who subjected them, who ruled over earth and heaven alike, bringing every thing under their sway. You may read in the splendid stanzas of the Book of Dzyan, as given us by H. P. B., hints of that mighty struggle of which the Purâṇas are so full, a struggle which was as real as any struggle of later days, an absolute historical fact that many of us have seen. We are instructed over and over again of a frightful conflict of forms, the forms of the past, monstrous in their strength and in their outline, against whom the Sons of Light were battling, against whom the great Lords of the Flame came down. One of these conflicts, the greatest of all, is given in the story of the Avatâra known as that of Narasimha—the Man-Lion. You know the story; what Hindu does not know the story of Prahlâda? In him we have typified the dawning spirituality which is to show in the higher races of Daityas as they pass on into definite human evolution, and their form gives way that sexual man may be born. I need not dwell on that familiar story of the devotee of Viṣhṇu; how his Daitya father strove to kill him because the name of Hari was ever on his lips; how he strove to slay him, with a sword, and the sword fell broken from the neck of the child; how then he tried to poison him, and Viṣhṇu appeared and ate first of the poisoned rice, so that the boy might eat it with the name of Hari on his lips; how his father strove to slay him by the furious elephant, by the fang of the serpent, by throwing him over a precipice, and by crushing him under a stone. But ever the cry of "Hari, Hari," brought deliverance, for in the elephant, in the fang of the serpent, in the precipice, and in the stone, Hari was ever present, and his devotee was safe in that presence: how finally when the father, challenging the omnipresence of the Deity, pointed to the stone pillar and said in mocking language: "Is your Hari also in the pillar?" "Hari, Hari," cried the boy, and the pillar burst asunder, and the mighty form came forth and slew the Daitya that doubted, in order that he might learn the omnipresence of the Supreme. A story? facts, not fiction; truth, not imagination; and if you could look back to the time of those struggles, there would seem to you nothing strange or abnormal in the story; for you would see it repeated with less vividness in the smaller struggles where the Sons of the Fire were purging and redeeming the earth, in order that the later human evolution might take place.

We pass from those four Avatâras, every one of which comes within what is called the Satya Yuga of the earth—not of the race remember, not the smaller cycle, but of the earth—the Satya Yuga of the earth as a whole, when periods of time were of immense length, and when progress was marvellously slow. Then we come to the next age, that which we call the Treta Yuga, that which is, in the theosophical chronology—and I put the two together in order that students may be able to work their way out in detail—the middle of the third Root Race, when humanity receives the light from above, and when man as man begins to evolve. How is that evolution marked? By the coming of the Supreme in human form, as Vâmana, the Dwarf. The Dwarf? Yes; for man was as yet but dwarf in the truly human stature, although vast in outer appearance; and He came as the inner man, small, yet stronger than the outer form; against him was Bali, the mighty, showing the outer form, while Vâmana, the Dwarf, showed the man that should be. And when Bali had offered a great sacrifice, the Dwarf as a Brâhmaṇa came to beg.

It is curious this question of the caste of the Avatâras. When we once come to the human Avatâras, They are mostly Kshattriyas, as you know, but in two cases. They are Brâhmaṇas, and this is one of them; for He was going to beg, and Kshattriya might not beg. Only he to whom the earth's wealth should be as nothing, who should have no store of wealth to hold, to whom gold and earth should be as one, only he may go to beg. He was an ancient Brâhmaṇa, not a modern Brâhmaṇa.

He came with begging bowl in hand, to beg of the king; for of what use is sacrifice unless something be given at the sacrifice? Now Bali was a pious ruler, on the side of the evolution that was passing away, and gladly gave a boon. "Brâhmaṇa, take thy boon," said he. "Three steps of earth alone I ask for," said the Dwarf. Of that little man surely three steps would not cover much, and the great king with his world-wide dominion might well give three steps of earth to the short and puny Dwarf. But one step covered earth, and the next step covered sky. Where could the third step be planted, where? so that the gift might be made complete. Nothing was left for Bali to give save himself; nothing to make his gift complete—and his word might not be broken—save his own body. So, recognising the Lord of all, he threw himself before Him, and the third step, planted on his body, fulfilled the promise of the king and made him the ruler of the lower regions, of Pâtâla. Such the story. How full of significance. This inner man—so small at that stage but really so mighty, who was to rule alike the earth and heaven—could for his third step find no place to put his foot upon save his own lower nature; he was to go forward and forward ever; that is hinted in the third step that was taken. What a graphic picture of the evolution that lay in front, the wondrous evolution that now was to begin.

And I may just remind you in passing that there is one word in the *Rig Veda*, which refers to this very Avatâra, that has been a source of endless controversy and dispute as to its meaning; there it is said:

Through all this world strode Viṣhṇu; thrice His foot
He planted and the whole
Was gathered in His footstep's dust. (I. xxii., 17.)[1]

That too is one of the "babblings of child humanity." I know not what figure the greatest man could use more poetical, more full of meaning, more sublime in its imagery, than that the whole world was gathered in the dust of the foot of the Supreme. For what is the world save the dust of His footsteps, and how would it have any life save as His foot has touched it?

So we pass, still treading onwards in the Treta Yuga, and we come to another manifestation—that of Parashurâma; a strange Avatâra you may think, and a partial Avatâra, let me say, as we shall see when we come to look at His life and read the words that are spoken of Him. The Yuga had now gone far and the Kshattriya caste had risen and was ruling, mighty in its power, great in its authority, the one warrior ruling caste, and alas! abusing its power, as men will do when souls are still being trained, and are young for their surroundings. The Kshattriya caste abused its power, built up in order that it might rule; the duty of the ruler, remember, is essentially protection: but these used their power not to protect, but to plunder, not to help but to oppress. A terrible lesson must be taught the ruling caste, in order that it might learn, if possible, that the duty of ruling was to protect and support and help, and not to tyrannise and plunder. The first great lesson was given to the kings of the earth, the rulers of men, a lesson that had to be repeated over and over again, and is not yet completely learnt. A divine manifestation came in order that that lesson might be taught; and the Teacher was not a Kshattriya save by mother. A strange story, that story of the birth. Food given to two Kshattriya women, each of whom was to bear a son, the husband of one of them a Brâhmaṇa; and the two women exchanged the food, and that meant to bring forth a Kshattriya son was taken by the woman with the Brâhmaṇa husband. An accident, men would say; there are no accidents in a universe of law. The food which was full of Kshattriya energy thus went into the Brâhmaṇa family, for it would not have been fitting that a Kshattriya should destroy Kshattriyas. The lesson would not thus have been so well taught to the world. So that we have the strange phenomenon of the Brâhmaṇa coming with an axe to slay the Kshattriya, and three times seven times that axe was raised in slaughter, cutting the Kshattriya trunk off from the surface of the earth.

But while Parashurâma was still in the body, a greater Avatâra came forth to show what a Kshattriya king should be. The Kshattriyas abusing their place and their power were swept away by Parashurâma, and, ere He had left the earth where the bitter lesson had been taught, the ideal Kshattriya came down to teach, now by example, the lesson of what should be, after the lesson of what should not be had been enforced. The boy Râma was born, on whose exquisite story we have not time long to dwell, the ideal ruler, the utterly perfect king. While a boy He went forth with the great teacher Visvâmitra, in order to protect the Yogî's sacrifice; a boy, almost a child, but able to drive away, as you remember, the Râkshasas that interfered with the sacrifice, and then He and His beloved brother Lakshmana and

[1] See also I. cliv., which speaks of His three steps, within which all living creatures have their habitation; the three steps are said to be "the earth, the heavens, and all living creatures." Here Bali is made the symbol of all living things.

the Yogî went on to the court of king Janaka. And there, at the court, was a great bow, a bow which had belonged to Mahâdeva Himself. To bend and string that bow was the task for the man who would wed Sîtâ, the child of marvellous birth, the maiden who had sprung from the furrow as the plough went through the earth, who had no physical father or physical mother. Who should wed the peerless maiden, the incarnation of Shrî, Lakshmî, the consort of Viṣhṇu? Who should wed Her save the Avatâra of Viṣhṇu Himself? So the mighty bow remained unstrung, for who might string it until the boy Râma came? And He takes it up with boyish carelessness, and bends it so strongly that it breaks in half, the crash echoing through earth and sky. He weds Sîtâ, the beautiful, and goes forth with Her, and with His brother Lakshmana and his bride, and with His father who had come to the bridal, and with a vast procession, wending their way back to their own town Ayodhya. This breaking of Mahâdeva's bow has rung through earth, the crashing of the bow has shaken all the worlds, and all, both men and Devas, know that the bow has been broken. Among the devotees of Mahâdeva, Parashurâma hears the clang of the broken bow, the bow of the One He worshipped; and proud with the might of His strength, still with the energy of Viṣhṇu in Him, He goes forth to meet this insolent boy, who had dared to break the bow that no other arm could bend. He challenges Him, and handing His own bow bids Him try what He can do with that. Can He shoot an arrow from its string? Râma takes this offered bow, strings it, and sets an arrow on the string. Then He stops, for in front of Him there is the body of a Brâhmaṇa; shall He draw an arrow against that form? As the two Râmas stand face to face, the energy of the elder, it is written, passes into the younger; the energy of Viṣhṇu, the energy of the Supreme, leaves the form in which it had been dwelling and enters the higher manifestation of the same divine life. The bow was stretched and the arrow waiting, but Râma would not shoot it forth lest harm should come, until He had pacified His antagonist; then feeling that energy pass, Parashurâma bows before Râma, diviner than Himself, hails Him as the Supreme Lord of the worlds, bends in reverence before Him, and then goes away. That Avatâra was over, although the form in which the energy had dwelt yet persisted. That is why I said it was a lesser Avatâra. Where you have the form persisting when the influence is withdrawn, you have the clear proof that there the incarnation cannot be said to be complete; the passing from the one to the other is the sign of the energy taken back by the Giver and put into a new vessel in which new work is to be done.

The story of Râma you know; we need not follow it further in detail; we spoke of it yesterday in its highest aspect as combating the forces of evil and starting the world, as it were, anew. We find the great reign of Râma lasting ten thousand years in the Dvapara Yuga, the Yuga at the close of which Shrî Kṛiṣhṇa came.

Then comes the Mighty One, Shrî Kṛiṣhṇa Himself, of whom I speak not to-day; we will try to study that Avatâra to-morrow with such insight and reverence as we may possess. Pass over that then for the moment, leaving it for fuller study, and we come to the ninth Avatâra as it is called, that of the Lord Buddha. Now round this much controversy has raged, and a theory exists current to some extent among the Hindus that the Lord Buddha, though an incarnation of Viṣhṇu, came to lead astray those who did not believe the Vedas, came to spread confusion upon earth. Viṣhṇu is the Lord of order, not of disorder; the Lord of love, not the Lord of hatred; the Lord of compassion, who only slays to help the life onward when the form has become an obstruction. And they blaspheme who speak of an incarnation of the Supreme, as coming to mislead the world that He has made. Rightly did your own learned pandit, T. Subba Row, speak of that theory with the disdain born of knowledge; for no one who has a shadow of occult learning, no one who knows anything of the inner realities of life, could thus speak of that beautiful and gracious manifestation of the Supreme, or dream that He could take the mighty form of an Avatâra in order to mislead.

But there is another point to put about this Avatâra, on which, perhaps, I may come into conflict with people on another side. For this is the difficulty of keeping the middle path, the razor path which goes neither to the left nor to the right, along which the great Gurus lead us. On either side you find objection to the central teaching. The Lord Buddha, in the ordinary sense of the word, was not what we have defined as an Avatâra. He was the first of our own humanity who climbed upwards to that point, and there merged in the Logos and received full illumination. His was not a body taken by the Logos for the purpose of revealing Himself, but was the last in myriads of births through which he had climbed to merge in I′shvara at last. That is not what is normally spoken of as an Avatâra, though, you may say, the result truly is the same. But in the case of the Avatâra, the evolving births are in previous kalpas, and the Avatâra comes after the man has merged in the Logos, and the body is taken for the purpose of revelation. But he who became Gautama Buddha had climbed though birth after birth in our own kalpa, as well as in the kalpas that went before; and he was incarnated many a time when the great Fourth Race dwelt in mighty Atlantis, and rose onward to take the office of the Buddha; for the Buddha is the title of an office, not of a particular man. Finally by his own struggles, the very first of our race, he was able to reach that great function in the world. What is the function? That of the Teacher of Gods and men. The previous Buddhas had been Buddhas who came from another planet. Humanity had not lived long enough here to evolve its own son to that height. Gautama Buddha was human-born. He had evolved through the Fourth Race into this first family of the A′ryan Race, the Hindu. By birth after birth in India He had completed His course and took His final body in A′ryâvarta, to make the proclamation of the law to men.

But the proclamation was not made primarily for India. It was given in India because India is the place whence the great religious revelations go forth by the will of the Supreme. Therefore was He born in India, but His law was specially meant for nations beyond the bounds of A′ryâvarta, that they might learn a pure morality, a noble ethic, disjoined—because of the darkness of the age—from all the complicated teachings which we find in connection with the subtle, metaphysical Hindu faith.

Hence you find in the teachings of the Lord Buddha two great divisions; one a philosophy meant for the learned, then an ethic disjoined from the philosophy, so far as the masses are concerned, noble and pure and great, yet easy to be grasped. For the Lord knew that we were going into an age of deeper and deeper materialism, that other nations were going to arise, that India for a time was going to sink down for other nations to rise above her in the scale of nations. Hence was it necessary to give a teaching of morality fitted for a more materialistic age, so that even if nations would not believe in the Gods they might still practise morality and obey the teachings of the Lord. In order also that this land might not suffer loss, in order that India itself might not lose its subtle metaphysical teachings and the widespread belief among all classes of people in the existence of the Gods and their part in the affairs of men, the work of the great Lord Buddha was done. He left morality built upon a basis that could not be shaken by any change of faith, and, having done His work, passed away. Then was sent another great One, overshadowed by the power of Mahâdeva, Shrî Shankarâchârya, in order that by His teaching He might give, in the Advaita Vedânta, the philosophy which would do intellectually what morally the Buddha had done, which intellectually would guard spirituality and allow a materialistic age to break its teeth on the hard nut of a flawless philosophy. Thus in India metaphysical religion triumphed, while the teaching of the Blessed One passed from the Indian soil, to do its noble work in lands other than the land of A´ryâvarta, which must keep unshaken its belief in the Gods, and where highest and lowest alike must bow before their power. That is the real truth about this much disputed question as to the teaching of the ninth Avatâra; the fact was that His teaching was not meant for His birthplace, but was meant for other younger nations that were rising up around, who did not follow the Vedas, but who yet needed instruction in the path of righteousness; not to mislead them but to guide them, was His teaching given. But, as I say, and as I repeat, what in it might have done harm in India had it been left alone was prevented by the coming of the great Teacher of the Advaita. You must remember, that His name has been worn by man after man, through century after century; but the Shrî Shankarâchârya on whom was the power of Mahâdeva was born but a few years after the passing away of the Buddha, as the records of the Dwârakâ Math show plainly—giving date after date backward, until they bring His birth within 60 or 70 years of the passing away of the Buddha.

We come to the tenth Avatâra, the future one, the Kalki. Of that but little may be said; but one or two hints perchance may be given. With His coming will dawn a brighter age; with His coming the Kali Yuga will pass away; with His coming will also come a higher race of men. He will come when there is born upon earth the sixth Root Race. There will then be a great change in the world, a great manifestation of truth, of occult truth, and when He comes then occultism will again be able to show itself to the world by proofs that none will be able to challenge or to deny; and He in His coming will give the rule over the sixth Root Race to the two Kings, of whom you read in the *Kalki Purâṇa*. As we look back down the past stream of time we find over and over again two great figures standing side by side—the ideal King and the ideal Priest. They work together; the one rules, the other teaches; the one governs the nation, the other instructs it. And such a pair of mighty ones come down in every age for each and every Race. Each Race has its own Teacher, the ideal Brâhmaṇa, called in the Buddhist language the Bodhisattva, the learned, full of wisdom and truth. Each has also its own ruler, the Manu. Those two we can trace in the past, in Their actual incarnations; and we see Them in the third, the fourth, and fifth Races; the Manu in each race is the ideal King, the Brâhmaṇa in each race is the ideal Teacher; and we learn that when the Kalki Avatâra shall come He shall call from the sacred village of Shamballa—the village known to the occultist though not to the profane—two Kings who have remained throughout the age in order to help the world in its evolution. And the name of the Manu who will be the King of the next Race, is said in the *Purâṇa* to be Moru; and the name of the ideal Brâhmaṇa who will be the Teacher of the next

Race is said to be Devapi; and these two are King and Teacher for the sixth Race that is to be born.

Those of you who have read something of the wondrous story of the past will know that the choosing out of the new Race, the evolving of it, the making of a new Root Race, is a thing that takes centuries, millenniums, sometimes hundreds of thousands of years; and that the two who are to be its King and Priest, the Manu and the Brâhmaṇa, are at Their work throughout the centuries, choosing the men who may be the seeds of the new Race. In the womb of the fourth Race a choice was made out of which the fifth was born; isolated in the Gobi desert, for enormous periods of time, that chosen family was trained, educated, reared, till its Manu incarnated in it, and its Teacher also incarnated in it, and the first A′ryan family was led forth to settle in A′ryâvarta. Now in the womb of the fifth Race, the sixth Race is a choosing, and the King and the Teacher of the sixth Race are already at Their mighty and beneficent work. They are choosing one by one, trying and testing, those who shall form the nucleus of the sixth Race; They are taking soul by soul, subjecting each to many a test, to many an ordeal, to see if there be the strength out of which a new Race can spring; and in fulness of time when Their work is ready, then will come the Kalki Avatâra, to sweep away the darkness, to send the Kali Yuga into the past, to proclaim the birth of the new Satya Yuga, with a new and more spiritual Race, that is to live therein. Then will He call out the chosen, the King Moru and the Brâhmaṇa Devapi, and give into Their hands the Race that now They are building, the Race to inhabit a fairer world, to carry onwards the evolution of humanity.

FOURTH LECTURE.

Shrî Kṛishṇa

MY BROTHERS, there are themes so lofty that tongue of Deva would not suffice to do full justice to that which they enclose, and when we think of the music of Shrî Kṛishṇa's flute, all human music seems as discord amidst its strains. Nevertheless since bhakti grows by thought and word, it is not amiss that we should come near a subject so sacred; only in dealing with it we must needs feel our incompetency, we must needs regret our limitations, we must needs wish for greater power of expression than we can have down here. For, perhaps, amid all the divine manifestations that have glorified the world, there is none which has aroused a wider, tenderer feeling than the Avatâra which we are to study this morning.

The austerer glories of Mahâdeva, the Lord of the burning ground, attract more the hearts of those who are weary of the world and who see the futility of worldly attractions; but Shrî Kṛishṇa is the God of the household, the God of family life, the God whose manifestations attract in every phase of His Self-revelation; He is human to the very core; born in humanity, as He has said, He acts as a man. As a child, He is a real child, full of playfulness, of fun, of winsome grace. Growing up into boyhood, into manhood, He exercises the same human fascination over the hearts of men, of women, and of children; the God in whose presence there is always joy, the God in whose presence there is continual laughter and music. When we think of Shrî Kṛishṇa we seem to hear the ripple of the river, the rustling of the leaves in the forest, the lowing of the kine in the pasture, the laughter of happy children playing round their parents' knees. He is so fundamentally the God who is human in everything; who bends in human sympathy over the cradle of the babe, who sympathises with the play of the youth, who is the friend of the lover, the blesser of the bridegroom and the bride, who smiles on the young mother when her first-born lies in her arms—everywhere the God of love and of human happiness; what wonder that His winsome grace has fascinated the hearts of men!

We are to study Him, then, this morning. Now an Avatâra—I say this to clear away some preliminary difficulties—an Avatâra has two great aspects to the world. First, He is a historical fact. Do not let that be forgotten. When you are reading the story of the great Ones, you are reading history and not fable. But it is more than history; the Avatâras acts out on the stage of the world a mighty drama. He is, as it were, a player on the world's stage, and He plays a definite drama, and that drama is an exposition of spiritual truth. And though the facts are facts of history, they are also an allegory under which great spiritual truths are conveyed to the minds and to the hearts of men. If you think of it only as an allegory, you miss an aspect of the truth; if you think of it only as a history you miss an aspect of the truth. The history of an Avatâra is an exposition of spiritual verities; but though the drama be a real one, it is a drama with an object, a drama with distinct outlines laid down, as it were, by the author, and the Avatâra plays His part on the stage at the same time as He is living out His life as man in the history of the world. That must be remembered, otherwise some of the great lessons of the Avatâra will be misread.

Then He comes into the world surrounded by many who have been with Him in former births, surrounded by celestial beings, born as men, and by a vast body of beings of the opposing side born also as men. I am speaking specially of the

Avatâra of Shrî Kṛiṣhṇa, but this is true of any other human Avatâra as well. They are not born into the world alone; They are born with a great circle round Them of friends, and a great host before them of apparent foes, incarnated as human beings, to work out the world-drama that is being played.

This is most of all, perhaps, apparent in the case of the One whom we are now studying. Because of the extremely complicated nature of the Avatâra of Shrî Kṛiṣhṇa, and the vast range that He covered as regards His manifestations of complex human life, in order to render the vast subject a little more manageable, I have divided this drama, as it were, into its separate acts. I am using for a moment the language of the stage, for I think it will make my meaning rather more clear. That is, in dealing with His life, I have taken its stages which are clearly marked out, and in each of these we shall see one great type of the teaching which the world is meant to learn from the playing of this drama before the eyes of men. To some extent the stages correspond with marked periods in the life, and to some extent they overlap each other; but by having them clearly in our minds we shall be able, I think, to grasp better the whole object of the Avatâra—we shall have as it were compartments in the mind in which the different types of teaching may be placed.

First then He comes to show forth to the world a great Object of bhakti, and the love of God to His bhakta, or devotee. That is the aim of the first act of the great drama—to stand forth as the Object of devotion, and to show forth the love with which God regards His devotees. We have there a marked stage in the life of Shrî Kṛiṣhṇa.

Then the second act of the drama may be said to be His character as the destroyer of the opposing forces that retard evolution, and that runs through the whole of His life.

The third act is that of the statesman, the wise, politic, and intellectual actor on the world's stage of history, the guiding force of the nation by His wondrous policy and intelligence, standing forth not as king but rather as statesman.

Then we have Him as friend, the human friend, especially of the Pâṇḍavas and of Arjuna.

The next act is that of Shrî Kṛiṣhṇa as Teacher, the world-teacher, not the teacher of one race alone.

Then we see Him in the strange and wondrous aspect of the Searcher of the hearts of men, the trier and tester of human nature.

Finally, we may regard Him in His manifestation as the Supreme, the all-pervading life of the universe, who looks on nothing as outside Himself, who embraces in His arms evil and good, darkness and light, nothing alien to Himself.

Into these seven acts, as it were, the life-history may be divided, and each of them might serve as the study of a life-time instead of our compressing them into the lecture of a morning. We will, however, take them in turn, however inadequately; for the hints I give can be worked out by you in detail according to the constitution of your own minds. One aspect will attract one man, another aspect will attract another; all the aspects are worthy of study, all are provocative of devotion. But most of all, with regard to devotion, is the earliest stage of His life inspiring and full of benediction, those early years of the Lord as infant, as child, as young boy, when He is dwelling in Vraja, in the forest of Brindâban, when He is living with the cowherds and their wives and their children, the marvellous child who stole the hearts of men. It is noticeable—and if it had been remembered many a blasphemy would not have been uttered—that Shrî Kṛiṣhṇa chose to show Himself as the great object of devotion, as the lover of the devotee, in the form of a child, not in that of a man.

Come then with me to the time of His birth, remembering that before that birth took place upon earth, the deities had been to Viṣhṇu in the higher regions, and had asked Him to interfere in order that earth might be lightened of her load, that the oppression of the incarnate Daityas might be stayed; and then Viṣhṇu said to the Gods: Go ye and incarnate yourselves in portions among men, go ye and take birth amid humanity. Great Ṛishis also took birth in the place where Viṣhṇu Himself was to be born, so that ere He came, the surroundings of the drama were, as it were, made in the place of His coming, and those that we speak of as the cowherds of Vraja, Nanda and those around Him, the Gopîs and all the inhabitants of that wondrously blessed spot, were, we are told, "God-like persons"; nay more, they were "the Protectors of the worlds" who were born as men for the progress of the world. But that means that the Gods themselves had come down and taken birth as men; and when you think of all that took place throughout the wonderful childhood of the Lîlâ[1] of Shrî Kṛiṣhṇa, you must remember that those who played that act of the drama were the ordinary men, no ordinary women; they were the Protectors of the worlds incarnated as cowherds round Him. And the Gopîs, the graceful wives of the shepherds, they were the Ṛishis of ancient days, who by devotion to Viṣhṇu had gained the blessing of being incarnated as Gopîs, in order that they might surround His childhood, and pour out their love at the tiny feet of the boy they saw as boy, of the God they worshipped as supreme.

When all these preparations were made for the coming of the child, the child was born. I am not dwelling on all the well-known incidents that surrounded His birth, the prophecy that the destroyer of Kamsa was to be born, the futile shutting up in the dungeon, the chaining with irons, and all the other follies with which the earthly tyrant strove to make impossible of accomplishment the decree of the Supreme. You all know how his plans came to nothing, as the mounds of sand raised by the hands of children are swept into a level plain when one wave of the sea ripples over the playground of the child. He was born, born in His four-armed form, shining out for the moment in the dungeon, which before His birth had been irradiated by Him through His mother's body, who was said to be like an alabaster vase—so pure was she—with a flame within it. For the Lord Shrî Kṛiṣhṇa was within her womb, herself the alabaster vase which was as a lamp containing Him, the world's light, so that the glory illuminated the darkness of the dungeon where she lay. At His birth he came as Viṣhṇu, for the moment showing Himself with all the signs of the Deity on Him, with the discus, with the conch, with the shrivatsa on His breast, with all the recognised emblems of the Lord. But that form quickly vanished, and only the human child lay before His parents' eyes. And the father, you remember, taking Him up, passed through the great locked doors and all the rest of it, and carried Him in safety into his brother's house, where He was to dwell in the place prepared for His coming.

As a babe He showed forth the power that was in Him, as we shall see, when we come, to the second stage, the destroyer of the forces of evil. But for the

---

[1] Play.

moment only watch Him as He plays in his foster mother's house, as He gambols with children of His own age. And as He is growing into a boy, able to go alone, He begins wandering through the fields and through the forest, and the notes of His wondrous flute are heard in all the groves and over all the plains. The child, a child of five—only five years of age when He wandered with His magic flute in His hands, charming the hearts of all that heard; so that the boys left tending the cattle and followed the music of the flute; the women left their household tasks and followed where the flute was playing; the men ceased their labours that they might feast their ears on the music of the flute. Nay, not only the men, the women and the children, but the cows, it is said, stopped their grazing to listen as the notes fell on their ears, and the calves ceased suckling as the music came to them on the wind, and the river rippled up that it might hear the better, and the trees bowed down their branches that they might not lose a note, and the birds no longer sang lest their music should make discord in the melody, as the wondrous child wandered over the country, and the music of heaven flowed from His magic flute.

And thus He lived and played and sported, and the hearts of all the cowherds and of their wives and daughters went out to that marvellous child. And He played with them and loved them, and they would take Him up and place His baby feet on their bosoms, and would sing to Him as the Lord of all, the Supreme, the mighty One. They recognised the Deity in the child that played round their homes, and many lessons He taught them, this child, amid His gambols and His pranks—lessons that still teach the world, and that those who know most understand best.

Let me take one instance which ignorant lips have used most in order to insult, to try to defame the majesty that they do not understand. But let me say this: that I believe that in most cases where these bitter insults are uttered, they are uttered by people who have never really read the story, and who have heard only bits of it and have supplied the rest out of their own imaginations. I therefore take a particular incident which I have heard most spoken of with bitterness as a proof of the frightful immorality of Shrî Kṛiṣhṇa.

While the child of six was one day wandering along, as He would, a number of the Gopîs were bathing nude in the river, having cast aside their cloths—as they should not have done, that being against the law and showing carelessness of womanly modesty. Leaving their garments on the bank they had plunged into the river. The child of six saw this with the eye of insight, and He gathered up their cloths and climbed up a tree near by, carrying them with Him, and threw them round His own shoulders and waited to see what would chance. The water was bitterly cold and the Gopîs were shivering; but they did not like to come out of it before the clear steady eyes of the child. And He called them to come and get the garments they had thrown off; and as they hesitated, the baby lips told them that they had sinned against God by immodestly casting aside the garments that should have been worn, and must therefore expiate their sin by coming and taking from His hands that which they had cast aside. They came and worshipped, and He gave them back their robes. An immoral story, with a child of six as the central figure! It is spoken of as though he were a full grown man, insulting the modesty of women. The Gopîs were Ṛishis, and the Lord, the Supreme, as a babe is teaching them a lesson. But there is more than that; there is a profound occult lesson below the story—a story repeated over and over again in different forms—and it is this: that when the soul is approaching the supreme Lord at one great stage of initiation, it has to pass through a great ordeal; stripped of everything on which it has hitherto relied, stripped of everything that is not of its inner Self, deprived of all external aid, of all external protection, of all external covering, the soul itself, in its own inherent life, must stand naked and alone with nothing to rely on, save the life of the Self within it. If it flinches before the ordeal, if it clings to anything to which hitherto it has looked for help, if in that supreme hour it cries out for friend or helper, nay even for the Guru himself, the soul fails in that ordeal. Naked and alone it must go forth, with absolutely none to aid it save the divinity within itself. And it is that nakedness of the soul as it approaches the supreme goal, that is told of in that story of Shrî Kṛiṣhṇa, the child, and the Gopîs, the nakedness of life before the One who gave it. You find many another similar allegory. When the Lord comes in the Kalki, the tenth, Avatâra, He fights on the battlefield and is overcome. He uses all His weapons; every weapon fails Him; and it is not till He casts every weapon aside and fights with His naked hands, that He conquers. Exactly the same idea. Intellect, everything, fails the naked soul before God.[1]

If I have taken up this story specially, out of hundreds of stories, to dwell upon, it is because it is one of the points of attack, and because you who are Hindus by birth ought to know enough of the inner truths of your own religion not to stand silent and ashamed when attacks are made, but should speak with knowledge and thus prevent such blasphemies.

Then we learn more details of His play with the Gopîs as a child of seven: how He wandered into the forest and disappeared and all went after Him seeking Him; how they tried to imitate His own play, in order to fill up the void that was left by His absence. The child of seven, that He was at this time, disappeared for a while, but came back to those who loved Him, as God ever does with His bhaktas. And then takes place that wondrous dance, the Râsa[2] of Shrî Kṛiṣhṇa, part of His Lîlâ, when He multiplied Himself so that every pair of Gopîs found Him standing between them; amid the ring of women the child was there between each pair of them, giving a hand to each; and so the mystic dance was danced. This is another of these points of attack which are made by ignorant minds. What but an unclean mind can see aught that is impure in the child dancing there as lover and beloved? It is as though He looked forward down the ages, and saw what later would be said, and it is as though He kept the child form in the Lîlâ, in order that He might breathe harmlessly into men's blind unclean hearts the lesson that He would fain give. And what was the lesson? One other incident I remind you of, before I draw the lesson from the whole of this stage of His life. He sent for food, He who is the Feeder of the worlds, and some of His Brâhmaṇas refused to give it, and sent away the boys who came to ask for food for Him; and when the men refused, He sent them back to the women, to see if they too would refuse the food their husbands had declined to give. And the women—who have ever loved the Lord—caught up the food from every part of their houses where they could find it and went out, crowds of them, bearing food for Him, leaving house, and husband, and household duties. And all tried to stop them, but they would not be stopped; and brothers and husbands and friends tried to hold them back, but no, they must go to Him, to their Lover, Shrî Kṛiṣhṇa; He must not be hungry, the child of their love. And so they

---

[1] So in the *Imitation of Christ*, the work of an occultist, it is written that we must "naked follow the naked Jesus."

[2] Dance.

went and gave Him food and He ate. But they say: They left their husbands! they left their homes! how wrong to leave husbands and homes and follow after Shrî Kṛiṣhṇa! The implication always is that their love was purely physical love, as though that were possible with a child of seven. I know that words of physical love are used, and I know it is said in a curious translation that "they came under the spell of Cupid." It matters not for the words, let us look at the facts. There is not a religion in the world that has not taught that when the Supreme calls, all else must be cast aside. I have seen Shrî Kṛiṣhṇa contrasted with Jesus of Nazareth to the detriment of Shrî Kṛiṣhṇa, and a contrast is drawn between the purity of the one and the impurity of the other; the proof given was that the husbands were left while the wives went to play with and wait on the Lord. But I have read words that came from the lips of Jesus of Nazareth; "He that loveth father or mother more than me, is not worthy of me; and he that loveth son or daughter more than me is not worthy of me." "And every one that hath forsaken houses, or brethren, or sisters, or father, or mother, or wife, or children, or lands, for my name's sake, shall receive an hundred fold, and shall inherit everlasting life." (Matt. x. 37, and xix. 29.) And again, yet more strongly: "If any man come to me and hate not his father, and mother, and wife, and children, and brethren, and sisters, yea, and his own life also, he cannot be my disciple." (Luke xiv. 26.) That is exactly the same idea. When Jesus calls, husband and wife, father and mother, must be forsaken, and the reward will be eternal life. Why is that right when done for Jesus, which is wrong when done for Shrî Kṛiṣhṇa?

It is not only that you find the same teaching in both religions; but in every other religion of the world the terms of physical love are used to describe the relation between the soul and God. Take the "Song of Solomon." If you take the Christian *Bible* and read the margin you will see "The Love of Christ for His Church"; and if from the margin you look down the column, you will find the most passionate of love songs, a description of the exquisite female form in all the details of its attractive beauty; the cry of the lover to the beloved to come to him that they might take their fill of love. "Christ and His Church" is supposed to make it all right, and I am content that it should be so. I have no word to say against the "Song of Solomon," nor any complaint against its gorgeous and luxuriant imagery; but I refuse to take from the Hebrew as pure, what I am to refuse from the Hindu as impure. I ask that all may be judged by the same standard, and that if one be condemned the same condemnation may be levelled against the other. So also in the songs of the Sûfis, the mystics of the faith of Islâm, woman's love is ever used as the best symbol of love between the soul and God. In all ages the love between husband and wife has been the symbol of union between the Supreme and His devotees; the closest of all earthly ties, the most intimate of all earthly unions, the merging of heart and body of twain into one—where will you find a better image of the merging of the soul in its God? Ever has the object of devotion been symbolised as the lover or husband, ever the devotee as wife or mistress. This symbology is universal, because it is fundamentally true. The absolute surrender of the wife to the husband is the type upon earth of the absolute surrender of the soul to God. That is the justification of the Râsa of Shrî Kṛiṣhṇa; that is the explanation of the story of His life in Vraja.

I have dwelt specially on this, my brothers, you all know why. Let us pass from it, remembering that till the nineteenth century this story provoked only devotion not ribaldry, and it is only with the coming in of the grosser type of western thought that you have these ideas put into the *Bhâgavad-Purâṇa*. I would to God that the Ṛishis had taken away the *Shrîmad Bhâgavata* from a race that is unworthy to have it; that as They have already withdrawn the greater part of the Vedas, the greater part of the ancient books, they would take away also this story of the love of Shrî Kṛiṣhṇa, until men are pure enough to read it without blasphemy and clean enough to read it without ideas of sexuality.

Pass from this to the next great stage, that of the Destroyer of evil, shortly, very shortly. From the time when as a babe but a few weeks old He sucked to death the Râkshasî, Pûtana; from the time He entered the great cave made by the demon, and expanding Himself shivered the whole into fragments; from the time He trampled on the head of the serpent Kalia so that it might not poison the water needed for the drinking of the people; until He left Vraja to meet Kamsa, we find Him ever chasing away every form of evil that came within the limits of His abode. We are told that when He had left Vraja and stood in the tournament field of Kamsa with His brother, His brother and Himself were mere boys, in the tender delicate bodies of youths. After the whole of the Lîlâ was over They were still children, when They went forth to fight. From that time onwards He met, one after another, the great incarnations of evil and crushed them with His resistless strength: we need not dwell on these stories, for they fill His life.

We come to the third stage of Statesman, a marvellously interesting feature in His life—the tact, the delicacy, the foresight, the skill in always putting the man opposed to Him in the wrong, and so winning His way and carrying others with Him. As you know, this part of His life is played out especially in connection with the Pâṇḍavas. He is the one who in every difficulty steps forward as ambassador; it is He who goes with Arjuna and Bhîma to slay the giant king Jarasandha, who was going to make a human sacrifice to Mahâdeva, a sacrifice that was put a stop to as blasphemous; it was He who went with them in order that the conflict might take place without transgressing the strictest rules of Kshattriya morality. Follow Him as He and Arjuna and his brother enter into the city of the king. They will not come by the open gate, that is the pathway of the friend. They break down a portion of the wall as a sign that they come as foes. They will not go undecorated; and challenged why they wore flowers and sandal, the answer is that they come for the celebration of a triumph, the fulfilling of a vow. Offered food, the answer of the great ambassador is that they will not take food then, that they will meet the king later and explain their purpose. When the time arrives He tells him in the most courteous but the clearest language that all these acts have been performed that he may know that they had come not as friends but as foes to challenge him to battle. So again when the question arises, after the thirteen years of exile, how shall the land be won back without struggle, without fight, you see Him standing in the assembly of Pâṇḍavas and their friends with the wisest counsel how perchance war may be averted; you see Him offering to go as ambassador that all the magic of His golden tongue may be used for the preservation of peace; you see Him going as ambassador and avoiding all the pavilions raised by the order of Duryodhana, that He may not take from one who is a foe a courtesy that might bind him as a friend. So when he pays the call on Duryodhana that courtesy demands, never failing in the perfect duty of the ambassador, fulfilling every demand of politeness, He will not touch the food that would make a bond between

Himself and the one against whom He had come to struggle. See how the only food that He will take is the food of the King's brother, for that alone, He says, "is clean and worthy to be eaten by me." See how in the assembly of hostile kings He tries to pacify and tries to please. See how He apologises with the gentlest humility; how to the great king, the blind king, He speaks in the name of the Pâṇḍavas as suppliant, not as outraged and indignant foe. See how with soft words He tries to turn away words of wrath, and uses every device of oratory to win their hearts and convince their judgments. See how later again, when the battle of Kurukshetra is over, when all the sons of the blind king are slain, see how He goes once more as ambassador to meet the childless father and, still bitterer, the childless mother, that the first anger may break itself on Him, and His words may charm away the wrath and soothe the grief of the bereft. See how later on He still guides and advises till all the work is done, till His task is accomplished and His end is drawing near. A statesman of marvellous ability; a politician of keenest tact and insight; as though to say to men of the world that when they are acting as men of the world they should be careful of righteousness, but also careful of discretion and of skill, that there is nothing alien to the truth of religion in the skill of the tongue and in the use of the keen intelligence of the brain.

Then pass on again from Him as Statesman to His character as Friend. Would that I had time to dwell on it, and paint you some of the fair pictures of His relations with the family He loved so well, from the day when, standing in the midst of the self-choice of Kṛiṣhṇa, the fair future wife of the Pâṇḍavas, He saw for the first time in that human incarnation Arjuna, His beloved of old. Think what it must have been, when the eyes of the two young men met, with memories in the one pair of the close friendship of the past, and the drawing of the other by the tie of those many births to the ancient friend whom he knew not. From that day when they first meet in this life onwards, how constant His friendship, how ceaseless His protection, how careful His thought to guard their honour and their lives; and yet how wise; at every point where His presence would have frustrated the object of His coming, He goes away. He is not present at the great game of dice, for that was necessary for the working out of the divine purpose; He was away. Had He been there, He must needs have interfered; had He been there, He could not have left His friends unaided. He remained away, until Draupadî cried in her agony for help when her modesty was threatened; then he came with Dharma and clothed her with garments as they were dragged from her; but then the game was over, the dice were cast, and destiny had gone on its appointed road.

How strange to watch that working! One object followed without change, without hesitation: but every means used that might give people an opportunity of escaping if only they would. He came to bring about that battle on Kurukshetra. He came, as we shall see in a moment, in order to carry out that one object in preparation for the centuries that stretched in front; but in the carrying of it out, He would give every chance to men who were entangled in that evil by their own past, so that if one of them would answer to His pleading he might come over to the side of light against the forces of darkness. He never wavered in His object; yet He never left unused one means that man could use to prevent that object taking place. A lesson full of significance! The will of the Supreme must be done, but the doing of that will is no excuse for any individual man who does not carry out the law to the fullest of his power. Although the will must be carried out, everything should be done that righteousness permits and that compassion suggests in order that men may choose light rather than darkness, and that only the resolutely obstinate may at last be, whelmed in the ruin that falls upon the land.

As Teacher—need I speak of Him as teacher who gave the *Bhagavad-Gîtâ* between the contending armies on Kurukshetra? Teacher not of Arjuna alone, not of India alone, but of every human heart which can listen to spiritual instruction, and understand a little of the profound wisdom there clothed in the words of man. Remember a later saying: "I, O Arjuna, am the Teacher and the mind is my pupil;" the mind of every man who is willing to be taught; the mind of every one who is ready to be instructed. Never does the spiritual teacher withhold knowledge because he grudges the giving. He is hampered in the giving by the want of receptivity in those to whom his message is addressed. Ill do men judge the divine heart of the great Teachers, or the faint reflection of that love in the mouth of Their messengers, when they think that knowledge is withheld because it is a precious possession to be grudgingly dealt out, that has to be given in as small a share as possible. It is not the withholding of the teacher but the closing of the heart of the hearer; not the hesitation of the teacher but the want of the ear that hears; not the dearth of teachers but the dearth of pupils who are willing and ready to be taught. I hear men say: "Why not an Avatâra now, or if not an Avatâra, why do not the great Ṛishis come forward to speak Their golden wisdom in the ears of men? Why do They desert us? Why do They leave us? Why should this world in this age not have the wisdom as They gave it of old?" The answer is that They are waiting, waiting, waiting, with tireless patience, in order to find some one willing to be taught, and when one human heart opens itself out and says: "O Lord, teach me," then the teaching comes down in a stream of divine energy and floods the heart. And if you have not the teaching, it is because your hearts are locked with the key of gold, with the key of fame, with the key of power, and with the key of desire for the enjoyments of this world. While those keys lock your hearts, the teachers of wisdom cannot enter in; but unlock the heart and throw away the key, and you will find yourselves flooded with a wisdom which is ever waiting to come in.

As Searcher of hearts—Ah! here again He is so difficult to understand, this Lord of Mâyâ, this Master of illusion. He tests the hearts of His beloved, not so much the world at large. To them is the teaching that shall guide them aright. For Arjuna, for Bhîma, for Yudhiṣhṭhira, for them the keener touch, the sharper trial, in order to see if within the heart one grain of evil still remains, that will prevent their union with Himself. For what does he seek? That they shall be His very own, that they shall enter into His being. But they cannot enter therein while one seed of evil remains in their hearts. They cannot enter therein while one sin is left in their nature. And so in tenderness and not in anger, in wisest love and not with a desire to mislead, the Lord of Love tries the hearts of His beloved, so that any evil that is in them may be wrung out by the grip that He places on them. Two or three occasions of it I remember. I may mention perhaps a couple of them to show you the method of the trial. The battle of Kurukshetra had been raging many a day; thousands and tens of thousands of the dead lay scattered on that terrible field, and every day when the sun rose Bhîshma came forth, generalissimo of the army of the Kurus, carrying before him everything, save where Arjuna barred his way; but Arjuna could not be everywhere; he was called away, with the horses guided by the Charioteer Shrî Kṛiṣhṇa sweeping across the field like a whirlwind, carrying victory in their course; and where the Charioteer and Arjuna were not there Bhîshma had his way. The hearts of the Pâṇḍavas sank low within them, and at last one night under their tents, resting ere the next day's struggle, the bitter despondency of King Yudhiṣhṭhira broke out in words, and he declared that until Bhîshma was slain nothing could be done. Then came the test from the lips of the searcher of hearts. "Behold, I will go forth and slay him on the morrow." Would Yudhiṣhṭhira consent? A promise stood in his way. You may remember that when Duryodhana and Arjuna went to Shrî Kṛiṣhṇa who lay sleeping, the question arose as to what each should take. Alone, unarmed, Shrî Kṛiṣhṇa would go with one, He would not fight; a mighty battalion of troops He would give to the other. Arjuna chose the unarmed Kṛiṣhṇa; Duryodhana, the mighty army ready to fight; so the word of the Avatâra was pledged that He would not fight. Unarmed He went into the battle, clad in his yellow silken robe, and only with the whip of the charioteer in His hand; twice, in order to stimulate Arjuna into combat, He had sprung down from the chariot and gone forth with His whip in His hand as though He would attack Bhîshma and slay him where he fought. Each time Arjuna stopped Him, reminding Him of His words. Now came the trial for the blameless King, as he is often called; should Shrî Kṛiṣhṇa break His word to give him victory? He stood firm. "Thy promise is given," was his answer; "that promise may not be broken." He passed the trial; he stood the test. But still one weakness was left in that noble heart; one underlying weakness that threatened to keep him away from his Lord. The lack of power to stand absolutely alone in the moment of trial, the ever clinging to some one stronger than himself, in order that his own decision might be upheld. That last weakness had to be burnt out as by fire. In a critical moment of the battle the word came that the success of Droṇa was carrying everything before him; that Droṇa was resistless and that the only way to slay him was to spread the report that his son was dead, and then he would no longer fight. Bhîma slew an elephant of the same name as Droṇa's son, and he said in the hearing of Droṇa: "Ashvatthâma is dead." But Droṇa would not believe unless King Yudhiṣhṭhira said so. Then the test came. Will he tell a practical lie but a nominal truth, in order to win the battle? He refused; not for his brother's pleadings would he do it. Would he stand firm by truth quite alone when all he revered seemed to be on the other side? The great One said: "Say that Ashvatthâma is slain." Ought he to have done it because He, Shrî Kṛiṣhṇa, bade him? Ought he to have told the lie because the revered One counselled it? Ah no! neither for the voice of God nor man, may the human soul do a thing which he knows to be against God and His law; and alone he must stand in the universe, rather than sin against right. And when the lie was told under cover of that excuse, Yudhiṣhṭhira doing what he wished in his heart under cover of the command from one he revered, then he fell, his chariot descended to the ground, and suffering and misery followed him from that day till the day of his ending, until in the face of the King of the celestials he stood alone, holding the duty of protection even to a dog higher than divine command and joy of heaven. And then he showed that the lesson had worked out in his purification, and that the heart was clean from the slightest taint of weakness. Oh, but men say, Shrî Kṛiṣhṇa counselled the telling of a lie! My brothers, can you not see beneath the illusion? What is there in this world that the Supreme does not do? There is no life but His, no Self but His, nothing save His life through all His universe; and every act is His act, when you go back to the ultimates. He had warned them of that truth. "I" He said, "am the gambling of the cheat," as well as the chants of the Veda. Strange lesson, and hard to learn, and yet true. For at every stage of evolution there is a lesson to be learnt. He teaches all the lessons; at each point of growth the next step is to be taken, and very often that step is the experiencing of evil, in order that suffering may burn the desire for evil out of the very heart. And just as the knife of the surgeon is different from the knife of the murderer, although both may pierce the human flesh, the one cutting to cure, the other to slay; so is the sharp knife of the Supreme, when by experience of evil and consequent pain He purifies the man, different, because the motive is other than the doing of evil to gratify passion, the stepping aside from righteousness in order to please the lower nature.

Last of all He shows himself as the Supreme; there is the Vaiṣhṇava form, the universal form, the form that contains the universe. But still more is the Supreme seen in the profound wisdom of the teaching, in the steadfastness of His walk through life. Does it sound strange to say that God is seen more in the latter than the former, that the outer form that contains the universe is less divine than the perfect steadfast nature, swerving neither to the right hand nor the left? Read that life again with this thought in your mind, of one purpose followed to its end no matter what forces might play on the other side, and its greatness may appear.

What did He come to do? He came to give the last lesson to the Kshattriya caste of India, and to open India to the world. Many lessons had been given to that great caste. We know that twenty-one times they had been cut off, and yet re-established. We know that Shrî Râma had shown the perfect life of Kshattriya, as an example that they might follow. They would not learn the lesson, either by destruction or by love. They would not follow the example either from fear or from admiration. Then their hour struck on the bell of Heaven, the knell of the Kshattriya caste. He came to sweep away that caste and to leave only scattered remnants of it, dotted over the Indian soil. It had been the sword of India, the iron wall that ringed her round. He came to shiver that wall into pieces, and to break the sword that it might not strike again. It had been used to oppress instead of to protect. It had been used for tyranny instead of for justice. Therefore he who gave it brake it, till men should learn by suffering what they would not learn by precept. And on the field of Kuru, the Kshattriya caste fought its last great battle; none were left of all that mighty host save a handful, when the fighting was over. Never has the caste recovered from Kurukshetra. It has not utterly disappeared. In some districts we find families belonging to it; but you know well enough that as a caste in most parts of modern India, you are hard put to find it. Why in the great counsels of the world's welfare was this done? Not only to teach a lesson for all time to kings and rulers, that if they would not govern aright they should not govern at all; but also to lay India open to the world.

How strange that sounds! To lay her open to invasion? He who loved her to lay her open to conquest? He who had consecrated her, He who had hallowed her plains and forests by His treading, and whose voice had rung through her land? Aye, for He judges not as man judges, and He sees the end from the beginning. India as she was of old, kept isolated from all the world, was so kept that she might have the treasure of spiritual knowledge poured into her and make a vessel for the containing. But when you fill the vessel, you do not then put that vessel high away on a shelf, and leave men thirsting for the liquid that it contains. The mighty One filled His Indian vessel with the water of spiritual knowledge, and at last the time came when that water should be poured out for the quenching of the thirst of the world, and should not be left only for the quenching of the thirst of a single nation, for the use of a single people. Therefore the Lover of men came, in order that the water of life might be poured out; He broke down the wall, so that the foreigner might overstep her borders. The Greeks swept in, the Mussulmâns swept in, invasion after invasion, invasion after invasion, until the conquerors who now rule India were the latest in time. Do you see in that only decay, only misery, only that India is under a curse? Ah no, my brothers! That which seems a curse for the time is for the world's healing and the world's blessing; and India may well suffer for a time in order that the world may be redeemed.

What does it mean? I am not speaking politically, but from the standpoint of a spiritual student, who is trying to understand how the evolution of the race goes on. The people who last conquered India, who now rule her as governors, are the people whose language is the most widely spread of all the languages of the world, and it is likely to become the world's language. It belongs not only to that little island of Britain, it belongs also to the great continent of America, to the great continent of Australia. It has spread from land to land, until that one tongue is the tongue most widely understood amongst all the peoples of the world. Other nations are beginning to learn it, because business and trade and even diplomacy are beginning to be carried on in that English speech. What wonder then that the Supreme should send to India this nation whose language is becoming the world-language, and lay her open to be held as part of that world-wide empire, in order that her Scriptures, translated into the most widely spoken language, may help the whole human family and purify and spiritualise the hearts of all His sons.

There is the deepest object of His coming, to prepare the spiritualisation of the world. It is not enough that one nation shall be spiritual; it is not enough that one country shall have wisdom; it is not enough that one land, however mighty and however beloved—and do not I love India as few of you love her?—it is not enough that she should have the gold of spiritual truth, and the rest of the world be paupers begging for a coin. No; far better that for a time she should sink in the scale of nations, in order that what she cannot do for herself may be done by divine agencies that are ever guiding the evolution of the world. Thus what from outside looks as conquest and subjection, to the eye of the spirit looks as the opening of the spiritual temple, so that all the nations may come in and learn.

Only that leaves to you a duty, a responsibility. I hear so much, I have spoken so often, of the descendants of Ṛishis and of the blood of the Ṛishis in your veins. True, but not enough. If you are again to be what Shrî Kṛishṇa means you to be in His eternal counsels, the Brâhmaṇa of nations, the teacher of divine truth, the mouth through which the Gods speak in the ears of men, then the Indian nation must purify itself, then the Indian nation must spiritualise itself. Shall your Scriptures spiritualise the whole world while you remain unspiritual? Shall the wisdom of the Ṛishis go out to Mlechchas in every part of the world, and they learn and profit by it, while you, the physical descendants of the Ṛishis, know not your own literature and love it even less than you know? That is the great lesson with which I would fain close. So true is this, that, in order to gain teachers of the Brahmavidyâ which belongs to this land by right of birth, the great Ṛishis have had to send some of their children to other lands in order that they may come back to teach your own religion amidst your people. Shall it not be that this shame shall come to an end? Shall it not be that there are some among you that shall lead again the old spiritual life, and follow and love the Lord? Shall it not be, not only here and there, but at last that the whole nation shall show the power of Shrî Kṛiṣhṇa in His life incarnated amongst you, which would really be greater than any special Avatâra? May we not hope and pray that His Avatâra shall be the nation that incarnates His knowledge, His love, His universal brotherliness to every man that treads the soil of earth? Away with the walls of separation, with the disdain and contempt and hatred that divide Indian from Indian, and India from the rest of the world. Let our motto from this time forward be the motto of Shrî Kṛiṣhṇa, that as He meets men on any road, so we will walk beside them on any road as well, for all roads are His. There is no road which He does not tread, and if we follow the Beloved who leads us, we must walk as He walks.

PEACE TO ALL BEINGS.

www.ingramcontent.com/pod-product-compliance
Lightning Source LLC
LaVergne TN
LVHW010939100826
845153LV00001B/93
* 9 7 8 1 9 1 6 9 2 3 6 1 4 *

An Interview with Gerard Wayland-Smith Jr.:

Conducted by Maren Lockwood Carden

Compiled by
Laura Wayland-Smith Hatch

Oneida Community Mansion House

An Interview with Gerard Wayland-Smith Jr.: Conducted by Maren Lockwood Carden
Laura Wayland-Smith Hatch, compiler

First Edition

All photographs are owned by and from the collection of Laura Wayland-Smith Hatch.

Copyright © 2026 by Oneida Community Mansion House. All rights reserved. No part of this book may be reproduced by any means without the written consent of the Oneida Community Mansion House.

Published as a gift for Oneida Community Mansion House by:
Salmon Creek Publishing
7580 Salmon Creek Road
Williamson, NY 14589-9510

ISBN: 978-0-9716794-6-7

Introduction

In the summer of 1961, sociologist and researcher Maren Lockwood Carden sat down with Gerard "Dard" Wayland-Smith Jr. to capture a piece of living history.

Their conversation unfolded over two sessions in the second-floor apartment of the Sherrill home Dard shared with his wife, Carol Gibson Wayland-Smith, and their two oldest children, Laura and Scott. The house, situated on the southwest corner of Sherrill Rd. and Hamilton Ave., had been built three generations earlier by Dard's great-grandparents, Francis and Cornelia (née Worden) Wayland-Smith.

Francis and Cornelia (née Worden) Wayland-Smith House, 1960

Originally preserved on magnetic tape and then transcribed onto delicate onion-skin paper, the interview records have been carefully digitized by Dard's daughter, Laura Wayland-Smith Hatch. Her work ensures that her father's voice and his part in the legacy of the Oneida Community and Oneida Ltd. remain accessible to future generations.

Throughout the text, Laura has included supplemental notes to provide broader context and share details that only a family member could offer.

Interview – Part 1

MAREN: Actually, you're the 3rd, aren't you?

GERARD: Yes, I am. [Note: Dard was born in 1934, a year after his grandfather, the original Gerard Wayland-Smith—an Oneida Community stirpicult—died. For that reason, his parents decided to use Jr. instead of the 3rd. Less pretentious was their thought.]

MAREN: How long have you lived in Kenwood?

GERARD: Well, I was born in Oneida in 1934 and lived here for—I think it was about four or five years. And then my father was a salesman for the company and we went on the road to Ohio and two places in Pennsylvania [including Bryn Mawr, where his younger brother was born] and then on Long Island. We lived there for a while.

Then, when the war broke out, they called in all the salesmen and we moved back in the middle of 1942 and lived here up until 1954 and in 1954 moved to New York [Note: Dard married Carol Ann Gibson in June 1954, and they moved to Flushing, Queens, New York, as a young married couple] and spent a couple years there. And then over to Spain for two and half years, and we came back in 1958—in the winter of 1958-59—and lived in Syracuse for a year. And then it would have been, I guess the spring of 1960—March of 1960—we moved back here to Sherrill Have been in and out.

Dard Wayland-Smith, 1952

MAREN: We will come back to that in a little while. Could you in the meantime tell me about your education—where you went to school? Did you go to college?

GERARD: Yes, two years at Rensselaer Polytechnic Institute. I went to high school right across the street here [Note: Dard was referring to the old

Kenwood Park School that has since been demolished.]. That was the high school at the time and graduated in 1952 and went to R.P.I. for two years [1952-1954], and then we moved to New York and I took some night courses in New York City in calculus and public speaking. While we were overseas, I took some correspondence courses and that was the last schooling I've had.

I hope someday to go back and get a degree in some field. I don't know what it will be yet, because I don't know what my work will be, which is one of the problems I have at the moment. [Note: Dard finished his B.S. in Industrial Engineering at Utica College in the late 1960s.]

MAREN: What jobs have you held before you came to Oneida?

GERARD: Well, I've really covered the route. I've been a popcorn popper in a popcorn factory in downtown Oneida—Jax Snacks. I've worked on an assembly line making school buses in Canastota. I spent a couple years in New York with Trans World Airlines—worked in their Reservations Department.

Overseas, I don't know what you would really call it. The title was "dispatcher," but it included a lot of other work. I took care of spare parts and maintenance and construction machinery and scheduling of maintenance. I had a number of Spaniards working for me. [Note: Dard worked for an international construction firm, Lummus Construction, building a NATO submarine base in El Ferrol del Caldillo, Galicia, Spain.]

Then we came back to this country and I sold automobiles in Syracuse. After that, I sold construction machinery for a while and after that I came to work for Oneida, Ltd., and I am now a trainee.

MAREN: Does the management have a trainee program?

GERARD: Well, technically the title is Home Office Trainee, which is in effect management trainee. At least I hope it's management training.

MAREN: Is this the same position that John Barron and Jim Allen hold?

GERARD: Yes.

MAREN: It is technically called "Home Office Training."

GERARD: We are being trained to work in the home office. This differentiates us from the sales trainees who are trained to go out on the road. It is a three-year program, as the other fellows have probably told you, and covers all sorts of different jobs–anything that they feel might be useful to you.

MAREN: Can you tell me why you decided to come back to Oneida?

GERARD: Well, it would be quite a long story. One reason was I was hungry and wanted to get out of sales, which I was in before I came here. I enjoyed being in construction work very much, but because of children I wanted to get out of that. There is a great deal of moving involved in that, and the kids were ready to start school.

MAREN: Your whole family would have had to move?

GERARD: Yes, as an example, we lived in Spain and the city we were in, there were no schools for American children at all, and we would have had to send the kids about 450 miles away to Madrid to school, which you just don't do with a six-year-old child. At least, I don't think you do it with a six-year-old child, and having grown up in Oneida and having liked it here—it is a very friendly town I always felt—and Carol always enjoyed it in the time she had spent here.

Carol, Laura, & Dard Wayland-Smith
El Ferrol del Caldillo, Spain, 1956

[That's] why I came down and spoke to Pete Noyes, and he offered me this opportunity with management training or home office training, and I feel that the training program is such that I really want to get into it. There is a good deal and [a] possibility of getting some place, so I grabbed the opportunity and came down to go to work.

As far as a real concrete reason, I think I would have to say a combination of reasons. I didn't care for the sales work I was doing in Syracuse. It was extremely long hours, and I wasn't that happy with it, and this was a good opportunity it seemed, so I latched onto it. Of course, the fact that my family is from this town, it helped me decide that much easier.

MAREN: Supposing you were going to get out of your job in Syracuse, what alternatives did you have besides coming to Oneida?

GERARD: At the time, I was looking all over Syracuse. I had been interviewed by a life insurance company. I guess General Electric and several other concerns, I don't really remember at this time. Previous to that, I had been contacted by several organizations in New York City, written letters and sent out résumés, etc., but I didn't feel I was getting any real concrete offers that were interesting.

As an example, the life insurance company in Syracuse. I don't even remember which one it was now. They gave me some interviews and said you're very promising material and so on and so forth, and I feel they would have given me a job, and a good job, but it wasn't the sort of thing I was interested in. I think that having rambled about the countryside that I more or less got a little tired of the banging around here and there and so on that you get into sales work.

MAREN: Is that what the life Insurance company work would have been?

GERARD: Yes, it would have been all sales, and I don't care for that sort of thing—barging into someone's home and trying to sell them insurance—and it is a high-pressure type of thing, and I just don't care for it. So, at the time that this opportunity became available, why it was the best thing, and as I said I was a little hungry. You have to eat you know.

MAREN: Did you just talk to Pete Noyes when you came down here?

GERARD: Well, I came down and talked to Pete. I'm trying to get it straight in my mind and just how it did happen. I came down and I think I talked to Ham Allen. Of course I've known Ham all my life. Ham discussed the thing with me, and he didn't know what they actually had open at the time, so I went over to see Pete Noyes, who I have also known all my life, and we sat down and battered around for about half an hour or an hour. He was very kind and gave me the time and he mentioned this home office training program and did I think I would be interested in it.

I went back home and discussed it with Carol and gave it some thought and finally decided that it sounded very encouraging. I liked the idea that you go into the training program and they are trying to fit you into a particular little corner right at the beginning.

As a matter of fact, I've been in now a year and a half and I still have no idea where I'm going to wind up with Oneida Ltd. I really don't think anybody else does, but it has been invaluable because I have been given the opportunity to visit any section of the Company. Everything is open to the fellows who are in the training program. Nothing is restricted in any way as to design or something of the sort. If we are interested in design, we can up and see them. They are very friendly and will try to help us cut in any way that they can.

There seems to be a great deal of interest in this program from the standpoint of the executives in the Company, and so I was very happy with the offer. Having talked with Pete, he really explained it to me, and I grabbed the opportunity.

MAREN: What sort of things was he looking for in his management training?

GERARD: Well, I really don't know. I have taken a series of examinations, various tests with the Company, the A.B.A.

MAREN: Can you think of any others?

GERARD: Oh, quite a number of them—mechanical aptitude and mathematical aptitude and that sort of thing. Several others I really don't know what they were. I practically don't pay that much attention to them. I'm not a firm believer in examinations. I've taken so many of them, these various tests given by companies, that I found that I can make most of them come out pretty much the way I want them to come out.

Take this life insurance company I spoke of before I took the series of tests for them. It was very interesting. A man told me he wanted me to take these examinations ahead of persons in the office, and I got to thinking about it. I had discussed with this man previously what he wanted in a trainee or salesman, and I went into the test and I had a feeling in my mind that I was doing exceptionally well from his viewpoint, and I had, yet I really don't think I had any great aptitude to sell. He told me I'd be a whiz-bang insurance man.

I've had this happen a number of other times, so I really don't have much confidence in them. The only one I've really seen that holds up is this A.B.A., which again shows very high in the sales, but by the same token I've taken quite a number of them. Let's see, for about seven years now, and they have changed radically, very much depending on what I was doing at the time and how I felt at the time.

MAREN: You mean that your responses change?

GERARD: Yes, the ones that I've taken, I've had a person tell me what they saw in it after they gave it to me, and I can remember one very distinctly. At the time I was having some problems about work or some such thing, and I was really down in the dumps, and I took the test. As a matter of fact, it was administered by my father. He used to give them, and I sat down afterwards and I said now what do you see in me? And he hadn't seen me for quite a period of time and he didn't know the problems I had with the work I was doing, and he told me I don't know that the problems are that you have, but I do know that you have problems in your work and you feel very depressed right at this present time. It was amazing to me.

Another one I took, I have forgotten what had happened. Oh, I know what had happened. I had just started selling construction machinery, and I took this test and at the time my spirits were very high. I was completely happy about the whole thing. Of course, I didn't know what I was getting into at the time of this examination or analysis. Actually, it was a test, [it] was one that I do feel was quite good.

MAREN: Well, then when you were taking the one, the various tests at Oneida, what were you trying to be?

GERARD: You see that there is where I get puzzled up. I think that probably they were the only series of analysis or tests—or whatever you want to call them—that I've been completely honest on.

From this standpoint, I really don't know what they were looking for. They sort of had me buggered up on the thing. If somebody sits down with you and on a test tells you personality test or something of that sort—do you like dogs or cats? light rooms or dark rooms? If you sit down with a person, and they tell you what they are looking for ahead of time, if you stop and think, you can pretty much answer them to their satisfaction. But when you don't have any idea what they are looking for, and the people administering the tests don't know what they are looking for, why it is pretty hard to change anything. So, I have to admit that I answered them quite truthfully.

MAREN: Nobody told you what they were looking for?

GERARD: Well, that's part of it right there.

MAREN: You mean there's more to it than that?

GERARD: Well, actually I think it is probably one sort of the examination (indistinct). I had the job at the time. There was no question about that. It's not as if you were taking a series of quizzes to find out if you were suited to the job. They were trying to find out something about myself for their own private records, and because of that it just doesn't pay to fool around with . . .

MAREN: Do you think it was an advantage to you in coming here, being a member of the family?

GERARD: (Indistinct)

MAREN: How much of an advantage?

GERARD: An important advantage. I have been in a position where I have had to hire people myself, and I realized this is an extremely difficult decision to make. And, if you don't know a person, you can only go by what you see on a piece of paper. It's pretty hard to make up your mind between one or two people, or should I hire this one person for this one function. This is a difficult decision to make.

I think if you have known a person for a period of time; for example, Pete Noyes knowing me, and Ham Allen. They've known me since about that high, and they actually, you might put it in the sense that they knew what they were buying so to speak.

It's a difference between going into a place and buying from someone you know and somebody you don't know. It's that general idea. They more or less knew me, knew my background. They knew the experience I'd had, but even more important they knew me personally, and this gives them a great deal of confidence. I'm quite sure that it was a very important point in my favor that they did know me well. Possibly Wayland-Smith didn't have that much to do with it. An Allen or Noyes could have done just as well. In fact, probably better.

MAREN: Can you tell me something about the new program—the new management training program? How many people are in it?

GERARD: Let me see now— Jim Allen, John Barron, Al Noyes, Bob Tegtmeyer, Ed Sitz. He's quite a fellow who has just [started] working for us apparently. He had been working for some college fraternity prior to coming here and is now in the training program. I don't know the details behind his hiring. I don't even know the fellow. He is way over in the night branch (indistinct). Walt Stewart, Gene (indistinct). There must be more. I'm sure I missed some. Bill Dowling.

MAREN: Of these, the last four you mentioned are (rest of question indistinct).

GERARD: No, I wouldn't say that. The majority of these people, Sitz no, he is not, but the rest, I think you would find their families have been in this area for quite a number of years. Not a member of the old community so to speak, but we have quite an unusual thing here. We have so many people with over

25 years of service, and in my mind these people are community people, the real backbone of our company. A person has to be awfully devoted to work in one spot for 43/45 years in a factory. They are really community people. You really have to call them that. They have done nothing all their lives but work for Oneida.

MAREN: Don't you really think these people (indistinct) families descended from the old community?

GERARD: Oh, yes from that standpoint they are not. They are not from the Oneida Community family in the sense that it has always been between the bridges. You've heard that expression, I'm sure.

MAREN: Yes, this little world between the bridges.

GERARD: Yes, it's a great expression.

MAREN: Why did you not like to be in sales since you have done quite a lot of sales work?

GERARD: This is a question that more people at Oneida, Ltd. have asked me. They have been trying to corral me into going into sales. Quite a number of people say when are you going to come and work with us in sales. I object strenuously to it. When I get done with work at night, it doesn't bother me if it is 10 o'clock at night when I get through work. When I get done, I want to go home. I don't want to live in a hotel. I don't care for the idea of constant travel, travel, travel.

Also, the only selling I've ever done is very different from Oneida, Ltd. selling. I sold heavy construction machinery, but this is something I understand, because I worked with it and always enjoyed machinery. The same with automobiles. I enjoy cars, and it's easy for me to discuss a car with a person. It has moving parts. You can show the quality in it from the moving parts standpoint. You can take it out and demonstrate it.

I've often thought, how do you demonstrate a piece of silver? Then about a year ago—a little over a year ago, the beginning of April, the end of Match—I had the misfortune to go on a special selling trip to Philadelphia Melamine dinnerware, and I have never been so confused in my life. It is very difficult to sell because you walk in with silverware or dinnerware and show it to a person; my personal opinion is that they like it immediately and want to buy it, like it immediately but they don't really feel they ought to buy it, or they dislike it intensely. There's nothing you can say to them after that point. That decision is reached. Well, the border line cases you might be able to sell, but I just don't know how you would go about demonstrating a piece of silverware. It's very pretty, very lovely, but the cheapest fork made will do the same job that the best one will.

MAREN: Were you successful on your selling trip?

GERARD: I was somewhat successful. We hit Philadelphia the very first, and I found out afterwards that the business conditions down there and selling in general in the area, was just terrible during the two weeks we were there. I guess from the standpoint of actual sales, no, we were not successful. As a matter of fact, I think you would say we were extremely unsuccessful, which I don't mean to be funny. At the time, it was quite a problem, and it was one of those things that I wasn't going to lose any sleep over it. There was nothing we could do about it. People aren't buying things, which is one reason why I don't care for sales.

MAREN: I thought they sent you down on a selling trip?

GERARD: As far as I know, it was a blitz type of promotion. They wanted to see what the effects of it would be in particular areas on four trainees. I mean to add to the trainees, Bill Dowling. He is a trainee who is now in merchandising. He was in sales training, and then in the home office training, and now in merchandising training. He often attends our meetings. I think you would say he is one of the training group.

We went on this blitz type of thing trying to find out what the effects would be if we moved into a particular area and just blasted all the stores with our promotion on melamine to get it going. You see, it was a new product, and nobody knew what it was, and nobody had ever seen it, and we really didn't have a sales force to sell it at that time. It is sold by our stainless-steel salesman, but it is only sold through a distributor, a wholesaler. The problem there is that they do not carry samples . So, you've got a new product. How do you get it to the retailer? All he's been seeing is a catalog. So actually, what we were doing was carrying the sample with us and showing it to retailers. We weren't going through the wholesalers at all. We were actually selling for the wholesalers, but, unfortunately, we weren't successful with it. It was really a crime, because I think we have a wonderful product, but I guess some of those things are human nature. I just don't know that much about it.

MAREN: What's happening to the dinnerware now?

GERARD: I guess close down operation. We are not making it anymore except in limited quantities. We have a tremendous inventory, or had one. We are selling it and apparently selling it on a nice, steady level from what I've heard, but it is nothing spectacular and doesn't warrant us to go at it hot and heavy again. So, at this point, we are running it as an extremely limited type of operation. We're cleaning out the inventory we do have, and the only manufacturing we are doing is to fill sets. We have the plates. We don't have the cups. That's about all we're doing.

MAREN: To go back to Oneida . . . Can you think of anything now that would make you want to leave Oneida?

GERARD: When you put that question like that, no. I am perfectly happy here. I have found the work to be extremely interesting. I know the people, and like them very much. My wife is very happy, and I can't really think of a nicer place to bring up children.

We have everything we ever wanted—beautiful homes, lovely lawns, good schools, the company is extremely liberal with its benefits. I've never given it much consideration, never worked any place where I could really take advantage of it. We have such things are our C.A.C. Clubs. It's really a wonderful deal when you stop and think about everything you're getting.

We have such a thing as Lewis Point. You've probably heard of it. A lovely summer club is what it amounts to with a limited membership. People, when you go down there, you know all the people, and it's an ideal situation. Prices are held very reasonable. We have, as far as I know, the only golf course you can join for $36 a year for the whole family. Unfortunately, we don't have a good clubhouse here. It's the only things we're lacking.

But, taken all in all, I can't think of a nicer place to live, and I've tried quite a number of them. I think this is one reason why I am particularly happy here. I think it would be hard on a person who has never left the town, who has grown up here, never worked any place else, never worked for other corporations or concerns and all.

And, frankly, it is the Company's attitude towards its employees that is amazing. I have never seen anyone who is so liberal, so willing to give the employee the benefit of the doubt, go out of his way to help him. We have such things as [a] Federal Credit Union. They've got so much money apparently, they don't know what to do with it, a savings type of thing.

MAREN: This is for the workers?

GERARD: Oneida Ltd. Federal Credit Union is for the employees. The only members are the employees and their families. You can go over there and get loans. The place is amazing.

MAREN: Can you think of any disadvantages of working with Oneida?

GERARD: I can think of one thing you happened to mention. The big (indistinct) between the bridges. This is always a disadvantage. When you get to know a group of people extremely well, and you are distantly related as I am to nearly everyone in Kenwood, you always get social problems, family problems. Someone is bound to get upset periodically. It's just like any family. You've got to spank the children once in a while. It's the same thing.

I really don't consider this a disadvantage because the same thing is true in other places, except in other places it is a great deal more impersonal, and I think this could hurt more than the personal side of it that we have here.

But, undoubtedly, there are disadvantages. You have to be careful of what you say, and you don't want to step on too many toes, because you know these people. They are actually friends of yours, and I think this is probably a disadvantage in certain respects, although it has never affected me at all. I would expect that some people would get very touchy on a certain subject. It may be a disadvantage. I don't know, but aside from that, and the fact that we didn't make any money last year, this bothers me more than anything else.

The idea that Oneida, Ltd., it is a tremendous corporation, has been in business over 100 years, and this is one reason why I was so happy to come back here. First of all, you have to stop and think that in my generation, my age group, there aren't too many fellows that did stick around. There are even fewer who went away and came back. I, fortunately or unfortunately, had the advantage or disadvantage of working in other places, seeing how other outfits operate, other companies operate, and coming back here now I can see certain problems that Oneida, Ltd. is faced with. Particularly the long-term employees, and we have quite a number of employees who are quite old. This hurts a company, but I feel that there is enough opportunity, especially right now. The sky is the limit.

MAREN: The sky is the limit for the company in America?

GERARD: I think that good work—really putting our nose to the grindstone—to more or less in my opinion clean house, like spring cleaning. If you clean once a week, you don't find much dirt around, but if you let it go all winter and clean it up in the spring—the place is awfully dirty.

We have had a problem in the late '40s and early '50s when we just couldn't manufacture enough merchandise, and we have built it up and built it up, and it has become very large, very complex and all of a sudden now—our business isn't horrible, it could be a lot worse—actually financially I guess we are extremely solid in very good shape. Of course, losing close to a million dollars didn't help any, but the sky is the limit for this corporation, and we have got to get our house back in order, and this is a difficult thing. As soon as you do start getting your house in order, you go back to stepping on toes of the family.

MAREN: That was going to be my next questions. What do you think of that?

GERARD: Well, I have only one concern. I was hired by Oneida for one purpose, and that was to do a job. I don't like the idea of going in and saying that this is necessary or this is not necessary, and Joe Blow who happens to be a good friend of mine is affected and all of a sudden, he doesn't have a job or something of that sort. You don't like that sort of thing, but it is one of those things that has to be done. My feeling on it, and I get it from working other places, not from working here. This is an opinion I formed many years ago.

My feeling is that the only way we can prosper here is to have the Company prosper, so that these steps that we take to make this happen are absolutely necessary. We have no choice in the matter. It is either do this or we aren't going to have a Company anymore. So, as much as it is disagreeable and everything else, it has got to be done, and I might have to be the one who does it. Why, if it wasn't m, it would have to be someone else.

MAREN: Well, how is it going to be done?

GERARD: I wish I knew the answer.

MAREN: Well, as I look at the firm, the top of the firm, and seeing as so many people know everybody else, I wonder how anybody can make any decision to dispose of several members of the family or people they've known for 40 or 50 years in management?

GERARD: I think you run into another problem here. Not just disposing of people—a cold-blooded term. I really don't think we have so much a problem of disposing of people.

In certain respects, yes, I think that one of our problems here is getting the utmost profit out of each and every individual. We can't afford to waste anybody's talent. We have some very talented people here. They have a great deal on the ball, but during this tremendous prosperity that we had right after the war, everybody could coast. We built up staffs of clerks and so on. This is an example of it. A department has grown from we'll say 5 people to 25 people, and basically they're clerks. We've hired a tremendous number of women—a great many of these women in the Sherrill factory—and really they are not necessary. We're not getting the work we need. They are turning out work, but they are not doing what I would call necessary, useful work. This is where we have gotten off the beaten track.

As far as members of the family, particularly those in the top positions, I don't think we can dispense with any of them. There is just too much talent there, but we've got to utilize the talent we do have much more efficiently.

MAREN: (Indistinct) the excess people in the lower level? Not management at all?

GERARD: I don't believe any company is ever rich enough (indistinct). I don't care who they are. I can't think of a corporation in the world that couldn't use better men in the top level, because this is where your decisions are made.

The routine day-in, day-out decisions can be made on a level much lower. Then you get down to the foreman and supervisors and that sort of thing. I would say that as an example in the factory, at the present time we have some very, very talented assistant superintendents, and this is the place where we are starting to really need the younger people again.

We're going to have a problem, in my opinion, in about 10 or 15 years with a great number of our top management retiring all at once. These fellows are just about 50 right now, and when they go all at once, we are going to be in trouble unless we've got somebody coming up (indistinct). I don't feel that myself, [that] I'm headed for any top-level position just overnight like that. Of course, I do hope to get pretty close to the top someday. I think everybody feels that way.

And in this Company, because of the age difference here between my age group, at present I'm 27, and the age group for the next big generation ahead of me, which is in the 45 to 50- to 65-year-old age group, they have nothing, just a big empty gap. This is where our problem is going to lie, and as from my standpoint this is an ideal situation. It makes it easier or it gives greater possibilities of going up faster. I think that this could be an extremely disconcerting thing to have happen because you may not be ready to go up fast. This is another one of our problems, to make sure that we are ready to go up fast if the opportunity should occur, or if it is necessary and, frankly, I look forward to that day.

MAREN: Is there any possibility of the top management now bringing in more people in this age group to be (indistinct)?

GERARD: Yes, again it goes back to the problem. Where do you find them? There is a tremendous depth of good, responsible, well-educated, well-trained, management-level people. It is true all over the country.

MAREN: Don't you think that Oneida has a great many attractions for these people?

GERARD: Yes and no. I don't know whether or not anyone has mentioned it before or not, but I don't know how great a problem it really is, but we don't pay the salary other corporations do. This is the big attraction today.

MAREN: Don't you think that the other attractions at Oneida can overcome the attractions of a large salary?

GERARD: Well, it's pretty hard to teach a person or explain to a person in a week's time or a month's time exactly what the advantages are. I think you probably know this is true and heard a million reasons why people like or dislike Kenwood, Sherrill, and the Oneida Community.

In my case, I've known what they are along, and actually at one point I think I gave myself a kick in the seat of the pants to get out of here just to find out what the rest of the world was like.

It's hard to explain to a person, and you have to be careful again from this standpoint. How do you pick good people because companies don't like to give up this top-level management? If they find out that something is going on and some fellow is going to leave, they want to know why, and it may be that can match or more than match the offers that we could make from the standpoint of pay, membership in various clubs, and that sort of thing as a business type of thing. Join up in a country club, and we'll put it up as a business expense.

It is a serious problem; and another thing, you might find that they are experienced management people, but are they trained for the silverware business? We have our own problems, as any other industry does. It's hard to say that you'll just go out and find people without a great deal more training.

MAREN: When you gave me your reasons for coming back here, you listed quite specifically you (indistinct) a job that it was a pleasant community and a nice place for your children to grow up. Do you think there is anything more besides this that you can't explain to an outsider who is coming into management?

GERARD: I'm sure of it. I could sit here and perhaps talk for the next 24 hours on the subject of why I like Kenwood, or why I like the Oneida Community. When you walk down the street in the evening and see the President of the company out in his front yard and say, "Hi, Pete. How's it going?" and he knows you by your first name. Dunc Robertson, the same way. You see him out on the golf course in an old shirt playing golf. Well, for instance, he played a game of golf with my 17-year-old brother [Bruce Wayland-Smith]. You just don't find that in other places. It is part of the charm or the benefit of living here, in my opinion.

I found it much to my liking as a form of type of life. You're not stiff or anything else. As an example, I'm a trainee in the company for over a year and a half, [and] Hank Allen is "Hank" and Herb Stoughton is "Herb." All members of the Board of Directors, Harry Farmer and fellows like that, they are all friends.

The thing that really intrigues me is that whenever you have a problem with your work or with your personal life or something of the sort, if you feel that some of these fellows can help you, they are more than willing to stop and spend one hour or two hours or whatever is required. It is part of the charm of living here. We could go on like this for hours.

MAREN: Can't you explain this sort of thing to others?

GERARD: I don't think you can. At least, I can't. I don't have the facility for words that others may have. It would be impossible for me to explain it to an outsider.

MAREN: Do you think that an outsider would be able to do that? That an outsider who came to Kenwood to live would be able to (indistinct)? Do you think that the outsider's chance of playing golf with P.B. (indistinct)?

GERARD: I'm sure they would. But I think that other people coming in here would always be a little suspicious of it. It would seem strange to them. When you are in daily contact with it, you don't give it much thought. This is why this whole thing is so intriguing to me—the idea of having someone come in.

It's interesting trying to find out what makes the whole thing tick so to speak. You just can't explain it. It's hard to put into so many words. It's not a cut and dry sort of thing. It's an elusive type of charm in this town, and I think that a stranger coming here, hired by Oneida Ltd. to work here, in a very short time would be on a first-name basis with everyone here.

But I think that for a period of time—what it would be I don't know, five years or what depending on the individual—but they would be a little leery of it. It wouldn't seem right to them because in most companies you know the floor sweeper doesn't say good morning to the president. He says, "Good morning, Sir." It makes a little difference.

MAREN: How can Oneida continue with this very democratic setup? How can the officials keep their authority?

GERARD: I've never heard any problem arise because I say, "Good morning, Pete," or "How are you?" because I know when I do something wrong, he doesn't hesitate to call me in and sit down with me and chew me out.

I may be strange in that respect, or different than other people around here, but as far as my work is concerned, I try to keep it as much as possible completely separate from my social life. I don't believe in bringing it home. I come home at night and discuss this and that in a vague sort of way, but I don't like to bring my work home with me.

This is true in other cases, but the idea that Hank would come in and give me the devil at 4 o'clock in the afternoon, and at 5 o'clock when I was leaving and walked by him, it wouldn't occur to me that he would be mad at me still. From a social type of thing, it just doesn't't' occur to me. I don't know whether this is true of other people, but it wouldn't occur me to think that, well, he's mad at me.

MAREN: If you had a similar situation in another firm and your boss got mad at you in exactly the same way, how would you feel about that?

GERARD: Well, first of all, I would probably never meet him socially. I found this true working in Spain. For an example, there we were in a town of 70,000 people and there were about 25 Americans. I guess I was about low man on the totem pole as far as authority among Americans was concerned, but I had about 12 Spaniards working for me. But I found there, surprisingly enough, a great deal more bickering and resentment amongst the Americans than I find here, and yet there we were. None of us having actually had ever known each other before we went to work there. But I think the reason for it was that we didn't know each other. We didn't know our dispositions, how we reacted, and we were put together and doing a job, and yet there was that constant bickering and battling—a social type of thing going on. Joe chewed me out and boy am I mad at Joe, and I wouldn't have him at my house for anything. I don't think I'd find that here. I am speaking very personally about this. This may not be true of other people. If it is here, I guess I'm just too stupid to realize it.

MAREN: Have you been bawled out for anything since you came?

GERARD: Really, no. I've gotten into mischief a couple of times—nothing serious at all. But I [think there is no] hesitation on anybody's part to let me know that I had done something wrong. I haven't made any serious errors, no. But even the minor ones, they don't hesitate.

There's an example in this training program. We go in and talk to the training supervisor, Ernie Dowling, at least twice a year. People that we are working for as trainees rate us, and Ernie calls us in, and I see Ernie three or four times a week. He's a very nice fellow, know him very well, feel he's as much a friend as a boss, and yet he has no hesitation about telling you where the weaknesses are, and I don't resent this at all. In fact, I may be strange in that respect, too, but I like a little criticism once in a while, because I know where I should spend my time and try to correct.

I think this is one advantage over working somewhere else. You come to realize it, that these things are not personal because in a big corporation—take Trans World Airlines as an example—and I cost the company $7,000 in one fell swoop, and believe me, they let me know about it, and it was a very cold, impersonal thing. You made a mistake, and one more of those and you are out on your ear.

I don't think here in this company, either myself or anybody else who was trying to do a good job would have been approached in those terms. There would have been a good chewing out, there is no question about that. But I don't think there would have been the "if you do it again you've out on your ear" type of thing that I got in New York City. Mainly, because they didn't know who I was.

There was no personal contact [with] the Superintendent of Reservations in New York. You just never saw him. You saw your immediate supervisor, and this was the only boss that you saw. The Superintendent of Reservations—the supervisors reported to him.

Here in a way, it is a little different. If it's a company problem, you will, of course, go to your immediate supervisor. This is what anybody would do. This is the only way you can run a company. But if you didn't feel you got the right answers, so to speak, you would eventually get to Hank Allen's office if you were working in the factory, or you would get over here in the sale office, and you might end up in Pete Noyes' office, if it warranted going that far. This is something that doesn't occur in other places. You don't see Vice Presidents in other companies.

Interview – Part 2

MAREN: One of the advantages of working for Oneida has often been said to be the security of one's position. Do you think your position is as secure as it would have been 30 years ago?

GERARD: That's a difficult question to answer because I wasn't here 30 years ago. I've heard about the good old days. I would say this—that right as of the present time, having just lost as I said before nearly a million dollars—that a person's security more or less depends on the moment, on just about how good a job they can do.

I'm speaking now of the security of advancing, doing better with your work, getting to a higher position, etc. I'm not now speaking of the security of working for Oneida. I think that one of the problems we probably have here, and it may not be a problem, is this idea that he's a member of the family so by golly we're going to find something for him to do, but you'll always find this. You just can't get away from it. It's one of those things, but I don't think that you will find that this is going to be as true in years to come for responsible positions. People are not going to be kicked upstairs.

Now, whether this happened 30 years ago or not, I don't know, but this is the reason it is so hard for me to answer your question. From the position of having a job provided, we don't lose another million dollars.

MAREN: Do you yourself devote a lot of time to your work?

GERARD: Well, I would say from the standpoint of time I have devoted to other jobs, no. This is the first time in my life I have ever worked a 40-hour week, and it doesn't occur to me to think that if I don't leave the plant until 5:30 that this is unusual. It's just an accepted thing. One thing I do try to do is spend the time I'm over there on my work, and in that way of thinking, yes, I do spend a lot of time on my work. I try to avoid wasting time.

As I said, the only really important thing to me when I go over there is doing the work required of you. That's the only way Oneida, Ltd. will advance, and that's the only way that I'll advance. And from that standpoint, I would say, yes, that I do spend considerable time.

I think that in this town you will find that a lot of after-hours time is spent devoted to talking about work, and I learn a lot this way. I enjoy it. I like to hear what other people think. You can't get away from it in a community as closely knit as this one. If you go out for an evening with somebody, sooner or later they start talking shop. It doesn't disturb me as long as it doesn't get specific.

MAREN: Specific?

GERARD: Oh, specific problems and the answers to it. General talk I don't mind. This I enjoy. I don't think you can avoid it. We spend the majority of our lives over there and the sales office, devoting it to one thing—how to make money. And you just can't put it down like taking off a pair of shoes. Once they're off, they're off. You just can't do that if it's not like running a light on and off. You can't get away from it that quickly.

MAREN: Do you like the (indistinct) of your work when it carries on into the evening.?

GERARD: I enjoy it. I don't think my wife does, but I love a good controversy. I'll start an argument with anybody over anything. I enjoy it from the standpoint that it's the only way I found to earn things. If I can get another person, whether I agree with him or not, to express himself on something, I can learn something from them, and I enjoy learning from other people.

It's an interesting way of learning, probably get the reputation of being a "screwball" and picking arguments. I don't mean to say I enjoy them from the standpoint of having a knock-down, dragged-out fight, but I do enjoy them from the standpoint that if can get somebody else who has an opinion on a subject to express himself, then I learn something. I get their viewpoint, and as you know there are two sides to every story.

MAREN: Do you think you could tell me what for you makes a good job?

GERARD: For me, a good job consists of having more work than I can possibly do, and finding out a way to do it. Really, to say a specific field, a specific type of work is what I want, I couldn't do it. I would hesitate to say any specific job was what I wanted. A job, to me, is most interesting when there is absolutely no repetition. The first time the wheel goes around. The second time it goes around, it's monotonous if it goes around in the same circle.

I like new things, different things, going from one thing to another, everything changing rapidly. I enjoy this type of thing. This is the type of work I like. As I say, I like to have more work than I can do and figure out how to do it. I enjoy being given the responsibility and then trying to solve the problem in a way that is satisfactory to everybody concerned without causing a lot of grief and strife and the simplest and the best solution for Oneida, Ltd., and again we have to go back to Oneida, Ltd.

I think this is one thing that I am extremely outspoken on. I don't believe in the adage of "I" from the standpoint of profit here at Oneida, Ltd. or any place else that I would be working. I don't know where I picked it up, but somewhere along the line I realized that if it's, well here's an expression that was given to me a couple years ago. If it's good for the house, it's good for me, and in the long run this is true.

I think they have finally come to realize this, and the only thing to really work for is how to improve Oneida, Ltd. and how to—this is the problem—how to make money. You see, we are a profit-sharing corporation. I would like to see those days come back. I think they can. It will take an awful lot of hard work. There's probably going to be an awful lot of grief involved in it.

MAREN: What sort of grief?

GERARD: From the standpoint of little kingdoms toppling. This is something you'd get in any company. People's ideas being rejected, and they get upset about it. Things changing. We're in a very, very fast-moving, competitive world today. We're not back in the world of John Humphrey Noyes, and we can't think that way. Change is a funny thing. People don't like it.

MAREN: Once the employees in Oneida, the management and the (indistinct), all had a great deal of trust for the management. If this change is brought about that you suspect may come, do you think that trust may break down?

GERARD: I see no reason for it. You can change. You can change fast. All you've got to do it tell somebody why, what you're trying to accomplish. I don't believe in keeping secrets from employees. There are some things in your work which you just don't discuss with those people. This is true in any job, any job with responsibility. You just don't discuss certain aspects of things that are going to come up, or you feel are going to come up, and either you don't have the responsibility or authority to discuss them, or you don't feel that even though you do have the authority that they should be discussed at that time.

I think for the most part, if a person is approached, told the change is going to be made, if you drop it right there you are going to be in trouble. A human being likes to be told why they have to change. [If] they can see a reason for it, then they're not going [to get angry.] They feel that somebody wiser than themselves or with more authority than themselves had decided this is necessary. They know what you're trying to accomplish, and I find this is true in my own personal work.

I use this method, maybe it has a little more salesmanship in it. Maybe this is what we have to have. On the subject of salesmanship, I really don't believe there is such a thing as a non-salesman who is successful in any type of work. When you have to deal with one other person, you've got to be a salesman. You've got to sell them your ideas, and the only way that your ideas are successful is to have them properly sold. I don' t think we'll have any trouble with the employees distrusting the management.

MAREN: Do you think this attitude of yours is held by other people in management?

GERARD: I haven't any idea. I never tried to find out. I'm sure it must be, because this isn't something I've formed on my own. This is brought to me by watching people operate, both here and in other places. Yes, I think this attitude is—why should we keep it secret? If it isn't necessary to keep it confidential, why bother? Of course, financial affairs and that sort of thing, that's a different story. But from the standpoint of we're going to change, this method of doing things over here is doing to be done differently. If we give them a reason for it, we don't have any trouble, and I think people here know that. People have to be sold.

MAREN: Do you yourself intend to stay in Oneida? Can you say this?

GERARD: Yes, I can give you a flat, unqualified yes.

MAREN: One more question before I move to Kenwood. You were telling me that one of the disadvantages, if you can call it that, of living here was being so close to so many people that you know very well, or that you were partially related to. Could you give me a specific example of how such a disadvantage might some?

GERARD: Well, as I think I mentioned before, this never happened with me, but I could conceive how it could occur. For instance, supposing you were in a responsible position and a decision has to be made. Well, as an example, taking some really abstract cases, I'm putting myself in a position which I don't aspire to at all. I don't have any idea of ever getting into that situation. I don't know how I'd handle it if I did. I think I do. I'm not really sure. I don't think anybody is until they have to make a decision.

Supposing I was in the Personnel department and my brother, seven years younger than I am, who is working in the plant as he is doing now. He works nights, and it came to a decision to lay people off. You can see where this could get to be a pretty sticky situation. He could get pretty mad at me if he felt that I was giving him the business. You could generate the feeling that you had gone overboard to help him or had gone overboard to be hard on him. It's pretty hard to find that middle road. This could be a conceivable problem. It's one of those things that I don't think occurs too often, but it can happen. It would happen a lot more in somebody like Pete Noyes' case than it would in mine.

MAREN: In Kenwood, are there any people you do not know by name?

GERARD: I expect there are.

MAREN: Could you make an estimate of how many you might not know?

GERARD: I would say that I probably can just about count them. I wouldn't say there were over 10 people, mostly recent arrivals. A fellow by the name of Rafferty who just came here off the road. I haven't had a chance to meet him. He is going to be a Sales Manager or an Assistant Sales Manager, and I haven't had a chance to meet the man. I'm sure that the first time that I come upon him, whether it be in his front yard, on the street, or at a social affair, that [I'll say, "How do you do?" and he'll be calling me "Dard," and I'll be calling him by his first name, which I don't even know at this time.

As a matter of fact, this is a great problem. There are so many people in Kenwood, many of which I've not seen for years, and it's hard for me to remember their first names and keep their names straight at times, and this can be very, very embarrassing at a social function, particularly when Carol is along, and I don't know how to introduce her.

Also, over at the factory, I think that I am probably known by 50 percent of the people working in the factory. Probably known either by name or who I am. I walk by people, constantly wave to them, say hello to them, and I haven't the slightest idea who they are. I am very weak on names. I can remember a face and know that I should know the person, but I can't remember the name.

MAREN: Could you tell me the names of your three closest friends here in Kenwood?

GERARD: I really don't know how to answer it. It's a strange type of thing. I've moved so much, so frequently. I've been living back here now for a year, that I wouldn't say I have any close confederates.

I seem to get along well with most everybody. We join other people socially, have long conversations, etc. I would say that probably there isn't another person any place that I would really call a confidant or extremely close friend. Of course, you take the fellows like Al Noyes, Jim Allen, John Barron, and people of that type, people in my training program. Very close to them from the standpoint of my business, my personal life. But I never felt a great desire to confide in people about my own personal life, never felt it was really necessary, so I just have never done it.

I don't mean to seem anti-social or anything, but I've always felt that maybe they're just not interested in my own personal problems. They've probably had a few of their own. As far as being friends, close friends, well for example, Al Noyes. Last summer at this time, he wanted to go down and pick up his fiancée's luggage, and he had no transportation at the time. He had no hesitation about asking me, "Can I borrow your car?" and I had no hesitation about letting him take it.

But as far as confiding in people, I don't care for it. I really don't like to let other people know everything I'm thinking. I don't know whether it's good or bad. I think from that, that I would be more apt to confide in older people. Not just from an age standpoint, but I think I find myself getting closer to them in this type of thing. Take somebody like Hank Allen. I know Hank quite well, have done some work for him. A boss of mine by the name of Elsworth Candee. I don't think you've probably ever met him or even heard of him. He's a consultant, and he's on a permanent retainer with Oneida, Ltd. I think I'd be more apt to confide in a person of that type, or with Ernie Dowling, my real boss. But as far as personal social friends, I would hesitate to say that I would confide in them.

MAREN: Considering your ordinary social friends here in Kenwood, you mentioned Al Noyes. Do you think that you have any friends that you are equally close to outside of Kenwood?

GERARD: I used to have, yes. A fellow in New York by the name of Sam Strong. If he called up tonight and wanted the shirt off my back, I'd put it in a box and ship it to him. Fellows I went to school [with], fellows that I worked in New York with.

You see, one of the things that I've gotten into in my various jobs is that I've been in places for just short times that it's hard to build up close friendships. There are three or four fellows scattered around the world in various sections that I would call very close friends. I don't correspond with them a great deal, but they're the type of friends I feel that if I happen to be in their home town and just passing through for the evening, that I'd call them up and I'd probably end up having supper and spend the night with them, but there aren't too many of them—maybe three, four, or five of them.

MAREN: Can you tell me whom you feel is the ideal Kenwood resident?

GERARD: I couldn't answer that. I really don't have any idea. I've never given any thought to it. This is one thing about your study that intrigues me. Here you are interested in something that I've never even thought about. I've accepted it all my life, and it's just impossible to answer such a thing. One problem that you have living in a town and being related to everybody [Maren's note: only ½ or ¼] is that not only do you know their good points, but you know their bad points as well. I would hesitate to answer simply from the fact that I don't really know. [Note: At that time, Dard was a blood relative to over half of the Kenwood residents. What Maren did not understand with Dard's answer is that whether or not Kenwood people were blood relations, they all felt and were treated like family, a legacy of the Oneida Community days.]

MAREN: In Kenwood and Oneida, Ltd., there are several newcomers, as you mentioned. Are you going to do anything to introduce yourself to them?

GERARD: Yes, whenever I see them, I'll speak to them. I think this is true of everybody here. I don't think that any newcomer or new person—well, as an example, the salesmen who have been on the road and really don't know the people of Kenwood—I don't think they ever think the people are shunning them because the people don't know them. I think you're more apt to find people walking up and saying hello, and I feel this way.

I will say this. I don't like to just force myself on a person. I wouldn't make a point, as an example, of having somebody moving into the town of going right over and visiting them, but at the first opportunity, whether at a party or on the sidewalk, I would say hello and introduce myself and try to strike up a conversation, or maybe over on the golf course you might join them for a foursome.

I'm constantly meeting people that I haven't known before. Putting in this pipeline over here the other night [Note: the pipeline ran parallel to the

Sherrill Rd/Kenwood Ave. bridge over Oneida Creek], and they had some machines going, and we walked over with the kids to watch it, and a fellow by the name of Frank Warren—you've probably heard of the Warrens—lives right next to Pete. Well, he was over there. I've never really known Frank at all, except to say hello in the hallway or something. Never had an occasion to meet him outside the office or some place, so we stood there and carried on a long conversation about how poorly they were doing their pipe.

MAREN: How do you decide whether a newcomer is a valuable addition to Oneida, Ltd. and to Kenwood?

GERARD: From what standpoint are you speaking?

MAREN: [Are they] suited to staying in Kenwood and working for Oneida?

GERARD: Well, in my opinion, the only thing that suits a person to work in Oneida is the job he does. This would be my only interest in him. I don't want to see the place fill up with a bunch of incompetents. [Maren's note: Everyone is (indistinct) on this point]

As far as social life is concerned, I would say that anybody can come in here. Not speaking now of the extremes to us, one side or the other—the loudmouth, the troublemakers, and that sort. They don't fit in anyplace. I think that any normal person can fit in here.

We're a large enough group so that everybody—there are enough different interests. There's a big group over there that likes to ski. I wouldn't get on a pair of skis in a hundred years. I think they are the most foolish thing I ever saw in my life. [Note: In 1942, Dard battled polio, a struggle that required six months in a body cast and several years in a walking cast. Though the illness left his left leg and foot permanently withered—ruling out sports like skiing—he remained incredibly private about the ordeal. He only spoke of his history with the disease when prompted by a question about his limp.] Doesn't seem to bother them any. I kid them about it, and they kid me about my fishing. They think I'm a complete nut on fishing, which I am. [During his recovery from polio, a neighbor taught Dard how to tie flies. He soon transitioned to the fly rod and became a highly skilled fisherman, undeterred by the permanent effects of the polio on his leg.] So, we're a large enough group that we don't have too much of that problem. There's somebody who has the same interests or generally the same interests in town.

MAREN: Some people say that Kenwood has changed over their lifetime. Can you look at your experience here in Kenwood and say whether or not you think it has changed any?

GERARD: Well, for me personally, I would say not a great deal. People have changed somewhat. Some of the old ones have passed on. There are some new people in town since World War II, but life seems to go on pretty much the same.

You've got the Mansion House. People are as friendly as ever. More or less the same rules and regulations apply, and you've got a happy group and a deadly serious group.

Things don't change that much. I don't think they'll change that much in my lifetime or in anybody's lifetime. I would expect over the period of six or seven generations, yes, a complete change; but from my standpoint, not in my lifetime. Of course, I can go back actually about 10-15 years, Things haven't changed that much.

MAREN: What do you do about any spare-time activities?

GERARD: I fish, hunt, tie trout flies. I like to fiddle with guns. I enjoy just sitting and reading.

MAREN: Can you tell me the names of the last two books that you read?

GERARD: *The Travels of Jamie McPheeters.*

MAREN: Do you know the name of the author?

GERARD: I can tell you in a minute. I have the book here someplace. Here it is. *The Travels of Jamie McPheeters* by Robert Louis Taylor [Note: a Pulitzer Price-winning novel], and the other one, *The Horn of the Hunter* by Robert

Ruark. I polished off the book by Theodore Roosevelt, the story of his safari through Africa, and magazines I pour through by the gross are all hunting and fishing magazines.

Basically, my interests are in the outdoors. I like to hunt, and I like to fish. I've done it ever since I was about eight years old. I've always enjoyed it, always seemed to stay with it. My brother has the same interests, and we spend a lot of time together Also enjoy golf.

MAREN: Any other activities?

GERARD: Well, golf is not what I would call an activity, not the way I play it. It's a battle. I don't have the disposition for it. I get too mad out there.

MAREN: What then makes you play it?

GERARD: I don't really know. One reason is that my wife took it up this year, and we joined the club. I keep battling away at it, but I'm not at all happy with the way I play. I hate to do things poorly. That would be about it, I think. I'm not interested in cards.

M; Do you belong to nay organizations?

GERARD: Yes, the local Rod and Gun Club. I'm also a delegate to the Oneida County Federated Sportsman Club. I'm certified as a firearms instructor for the State of New York and the National Rifle Association, pretty much organizations in that line. Not much of anything else.

I don't like to join an organization that I don't have an intense interest in because I feel I'm wasting their time, or my time, so I don't just see how many organizations I can belong to.

MAREN: Do you belong to a church?

GERARD: Yes, the Episcopal church.

MAREN: Do you attend regularly?

GERARD: Quite infrequently.

MAREN: When did you go last?

GERARD: Easter. I'm a very, very poor churchgoer. My wife is the churchgoer. She does the praying, and I do the fishing.

MAREN: Do you go visiting very often?

GERARD: Not a great deal. We get together with other couples occasionally. More apt to wind up playing golf with somebody or see somebody at the golf course, and they'll say stop by after you get done and have a drink, or just stop over or something of the sort. Very informal type of thing. If we do go visiting, it's quite seldom that you'll see anybody in a white shirt and necktie.

MAREN: Getting back to what you've read again, can you tell me what you have read on the old community and the later years.

GERARD: *The First Hundred Years*. I think everyone's read that. You must have a copy of that by now.

MAREN: Not of my own, but I've read one.

GERARD: You don't have a copy of your own. Goods heavens, we're slipping. Why, the company gives them out like mud. I think I have one here, and if I do you can have it and take it along when we're done. I can always get more. I think they print them by the bushel.

MAREN: They [give them] to the employees, do they?

GERARD: Most of them. The new employees, particularly the office employees. I don't think they do so much in the factory. [indistinct] I can't remember the titles. I've read most of P. B. Noyes' books, *My Father's Hous*e and that sort of thing. I cruise through the old copies of *The Quadrangle* once in a while up at the Mansion House, but that's about it. Frankly, I never worried much about the company in its earlier days.

I'll tell you a couple of books I have read were written by a fellow named Sewall Newhouse, who was the one who started the trap business. I guess he used to live right here in the house in back of us. I've always enjoyed his books, primarily because they were on trapping and that sort of thing—with the outdoors. That's about it.

MAREN: Can you tell me what are the two most important qualities you look for in a friend?

GERARD: I don't think I've ever picked out any qualities. I have more of a tendency to take people at face value, and I either like them— like them very well or like them lukewarm. I can't say that there's anybody that I dislike. I feel that it's not worth the effort to dislike a person because there are redeeming qualities about everybody.

I really don't think I could answer it and say one or two particular qualities. I've never given it any consideration. One reason for it around here particularly is that you've grown up with these fellows, and you know their strong points and their weak points, and you accept them and that's it. I don't think I've given any particular thought to qualities.

Naturally, common interests make you that much closer and make you get together that [much] more often and pursue the common interests such as fishing, golf, skiing, swimming, whatever it happens to be. But as far as the specific quality in a person, no.

MAREN: Can you remember any occasion when you have stood up for principle against other people?

G; I know I have. I'm just trying to think of a specific instance. Yes, I wish you could have a tape recording of some of the home office training meetings because I really do get into some beauts over there.

I'm extremely conservative. I guess you'd say of the Barry Goldwater school, as I've said earlier in our conversation. The only thing we are in business for is to make money. I don't feel that we're here just to provide jobs or just to make happy lives. This is a part of what we are doing because of the manner we're doing it in, but basically, we're here to show a profit. Our company is based on that, and if we don't, we're going to go out of business.

I've gotten into some rather bitter debates on just how we ought to go about it—what a fair profit is and that sort of thing. I'm quite outspoken on the subject, particularly when somebody says something I don't agree with.

Other specifics as far as personal types of things—personal thought, ideas, somebody social—you might say I try to stay out of that as much as possible. I don't feel that you gain any respect from anybody by tearing down the social viewpoints. I don't feel that it's so much a case of rearing up on your hind legs and bellowing at somebody. It goes back to the salesmanship idea when they say something and you disagree with them. It's a lot of fun to sell them on your idea, and I think that as far as the social beliefs or ideas, the raising of children by other people or something of the sort. I don't hesitate to speak my views on it, but I don't [indistinct], but when I get in a business discussion over at the company, particularly the training program and frequently with this gentleman I'm working with—this Elsworth Candee. I have no hesitation to give him my ideas on a subject. If he asks me a question, I don't feel that it pays to just say yes to him Sometimes I disagree with what he has to say. Usually he winds up right, and he can prove it, but it's all part of learning.

MAREN: You were talking about the suggestions?

GERARD: Yes, we call it our Thousand Dollar a Year Club. To become a member, you write up an idea that you feel would save Oneida, Ltd. at least $1,000 the first year, and we have one person and their only function is to take these forms which come in and track them down to see whether the idea is worthwhile or not. I think it's somewhere around 50 percent of the suggestions that come in are accepted, and yet we don't give one cent in recognition. We have a dinner four times a year. You can get a quarterly membership for $250, half-year membership, three-quarters, or a year. Nobody has more than a one-year membership. In other words, if you turn in something that's $10,000, it's still only one year, and the thing is just unbelievable. We have one man doing nothing all day long, forty hours a week, except tracking these things down.

MAREN: Why do people take the trouble to think up ideas and hand them in?

GERARD: I think it's the idea they are giving a little recognition and the dinner, and they are given a bowl or an award of some sort, but I've heard a lot of criticism that we don't give money. Most companies do. They have very worthwhile rewards for people, but the darn thing seems to function perfectly. I can't remember the exact figures, but it seems to me that there's been about a quarter of a million dollars' worth of suggestions turned in that have been accepted. The thing has been functioning only a very few years, actually. Why it works, I don't know.

MAREN: I can see some employee saying if I save the company $10,000, [indistinct]

GERARD: Well, this is true. They do get that, and yet year after year you'll get people from Henry [Hank] Allen, who is director of works, all the way to the janitor turning in suggestions. About all they get out of it is a bowl or some other type of award and a free dinner a couple times a year.

MAREN: Everybody goes to the free dinner?

GERARD: Members only. Most of the members attend them. They have very good dinners, streak. We can afford it for that group, but some of the ideas are very worthwhile. I can remember some of them that came in were worth $10,000 or $12,000, and people turn them in. They happen to be doing a particular job, and they find a better way of doing it, or they think they have a better way—a different tool or a different type of machine, or a different procedure all together for doing something—and they turn it in. It has become an accepted type of thing. They just fill out a form and send it to this one fellow who tracks it all down for you. People submit things such as a new design for holloware. They'll take existing ways and come up with new ideas. They've very conscientious about it. I'm quite amazed at it.

MAREN: One of the disadvantages found in that sort of scheme is that often an idea comes not from a single man, but from a group of men. Do you think that happens here?

GERARD: I'm sure it does, and it will be turned in that way.

MAREN: Will it be turned in as from one man or from a group?

GERARD: I believe it comes in from the group. Supposing two fellows got together, and they were doing a particular job, and they decided in their own minds that this could be done a better way, a cheaper way of doing it. You see, the only qualification is that it's got to save money. This is the only stipulation. Well, they would turn the thing in, and if it worked out, they would both get recognition for it. If it happens to be a thousand dollars, why probably they would each get a half-year membership. If it came to two thousand, they would each get s full year membership. As far as recognition, they don't hesitate in that respect if two or three fellows get together on it. It's quite amazing.

End of the Interviews

The Final Chapter - A Daughter's Reflection on her Father's Legacy

In July 1964, Dard and Carol Wayland-Smith transformed their Ford station wagon into a vessel for adventure. Packed with three children and a mountain of gear, they embarked on a six-and-a-half-day odyssey across the United States and the rugged Mexican desert and mountains, eventually descending into the heart of Mexico City.

Dard had accepted the role of assistant general manager at the Oneida Mexicana plant in Toluca—a position designed to immerse him in the core of the factory's operations. What was intended as a brief six-month assignment stretched into eighteen months after the general manager, Charles Marshall, fell ill. This unexpected extension did more than just lengthen their stay; it set the stage for a lifetime defined by international service.

After a brief return to Oneida in 1966 and a three-month dispatch to Northern Ireland—during which Carol and the children stayed with Dard's mother in Kenwood—the family finally settled into "The Vineyard" in 1967. The big yellow house was steeped in family history, situated next door to Dard's childhood home and formerly occupied by his grandmother and great-aunt.

Yet the pull of Mexico remained. In 1972, the family left Kenwood permanently for Dard to take the helm as General Manager and, eventually, President of Oneida Mexicana. While their eldest daughter, Laura, remained in the U.S. for university, Scott and Jennifer grew up in Mexico City, staying through their own high school graduations at Colegio Americano before returning to the States for their careers.

By the time Dard retired in 1991, he had dedicated 31 years to the growth of Oneida Ltd. and Oneida Mexicana. His impact was profound: he expanded the Toluca plant's reach across all of Latin America and channeled his passion for craftsmanship into designing custom cutlery. He became known for his specialized steak and hunting knives, utilizing the incredibly hard, beautiful lignum vitae wood for the handles. These years were equally vibrant for Carol, who started her own successful business in Mexico City. Together, they forged deep, lasting friendships that bridged their professional and personal lives.

For their final act, Dard and Carol traded the boardroom and the frantic pace of Mexico City for the quiet majesty of the Rocky Mountains. They moved into a log cabin they built themselves in Libby, Montana. It was a fitting conclusion: the man who had mastered the complexities of a global corporation found his greatest peace in the rhythm of a fly rod and the beauty of the Kootenai River.

When Dard passed away in his beloved cabin in 2007, he left behind a legacy of dedication—to his craft, to his company, and, most importantly, to the family who had traveled the long road by his side.

Dard in his retirement, fly fishing on the Kootenai River.

www.ingramcontent.com/pod-product-compliance
Lightning Source LLC
LaVergne TN
LVHW010939100826
845153LV00001B/94
9780971679467